WWW.ZODIACSERVICES.NET

Presents

MBA BASICS IN 24 HOURS!

A SIMPLE Q&A BOOK OF MASTERS IN BUSINESS ADMINISTRATION

ADDITIONAL BOOK 3 MANAGEMENT Q&A WORKBOOK

Q & A

Life Grows With Us!

SIMPLE & EASY WAY TO UNDERSTAND THE BASICS OF BUSINESS ADMINISTRATION TOPICS EASILY IN QUESTIONS AND ANSWERS WITH EFFECTIVE CHAPTERS & ADDITIONAL TOPICS!

By

G.R. Narasimhan

Welcome to Zodiac Services MBA chapters in brief with management effective topics and additional special topics given as Q&A book!

GOOD LUCK TO BE A BUSINESS ADMINISTRATOR!

Copyright © 2019 by **G.R. Narasimhan**

All rights reserved. No part of this book/e-book may be reproduced, distributed or transmitted in any form or by any means, including photocopying, recording or other electronic or mechanical methods, without the prior written permission of the author, except in the case of brief quotations embodied in critical reviews and certain other non-commercial uses permitted by copyright law. For permission requests, write to the author, addressed "Attention: Author," at the address below.

Zodiac Services, Chennai, India

Get more contact details and numbers from:

www.zodiacservices.net [or] mail to info@zodiacservices.net

Ordering Information for hardcopies:

Quantity sales – Special discounts are available on quantity purchases by corporations, associations and others. For details, contact the author at the address above.

OCT 2019 – First Edition

Released and Published in Amazon India

****
Legal Disclaimer/ Notice

All the chapters, topics, discussions, statements, e-books/books and web contents including this MBA in 24 hours either online or offline are under business administration category. This guide is recommended to get simple understanding and guidance of bachelors or masters in business administration only. Readers are requested to apply their own knowledge or refer or consult their own tutors or masters before acting on any of the recommendations for examinations and related activities. Neither Zodiac services nor any of its promoters, members or author (if anyone) holds any responsibility of any losses/ liability incurred (if any/ if you end up in loss) by acting on the same as given to follow in presentations or examinations. We or Zodiac services, Chennai/head or branch offices anywhere in the world, are not responsible for, and will not compensate in any way for, any loss or damage related directly or indirectly from/to the information on this book/e-book. Thanks for your cooperation!

****

ABOUT THE AUTHOR

G.R. Narasimhan – Sr. Consultant for technology and business under **Zodiac Services Chennai** (as on June 2019) which was started in 2010 to serve the people in alternative beliefs/therapies like astrological predictions, prayers, remedies, prasnam (divine words) and vedic guidance for short- or long-term problems, vastu, numerology, gem stones, yantras, mantras or rituals (related areas), yoga, meditation, counseling and alternative therapies consulting. Business & education, soft skills/software/electronics & communication training & promotion, web designing, career counseling and Internet & social media marketing are additionally served. Assisting the entrepreneurship business for the above mentioned areas to serve better for the clients, **G.R. Narasimhan** also the author of few e-books called "A Simple guide to Vedic Astrology," "Inverted Universal Meditation & Engineering," "Secrets of Equity Stocks to make Millions," "Symbolic Meditation & Developing ESP" and many other (are already available in Amazon) having extended experience in IT + Management areas developed website and online marketing using different business strategies and continue the service very well to extend further including this "MBA Basics in 24 Hours with Additional Topics – Global Marketing and Foreign Trade"; – "MBA Basics in 24 Hours with Additional Topics –Management Workbook with Q & A" concepts specifically based on the business administration topics applied overall in the academic/professional curriculum. With the continuous extraordinary ability and skills in research and experience, he is able to explain and train/assist others with extended support and guidance by counseling/consulting effectively.

Great thanks and good luck for everyone reading this book on "MBA Basics in 24 Hours" with almost all the areas of basic business administration or career growth individually or as a group. For any queries and feedback, you can contact directly via email to info@zodiacservices.net, info@astroservices.in or astronara@gmail.com.

CONTENTS

Topic	Page Numbers
Introduction	05
Chapter One - Multiple Choice Questions!	06
Chapter One - Answers : Mutiple Choice Questions	20
Chapter Two - Brief Questions	21
Chapter Two - Answers to Brief Questions	25
Chapter Three - Long Questions	66
Chapter Three - Answers to Long Questions	69
Conclusion	140

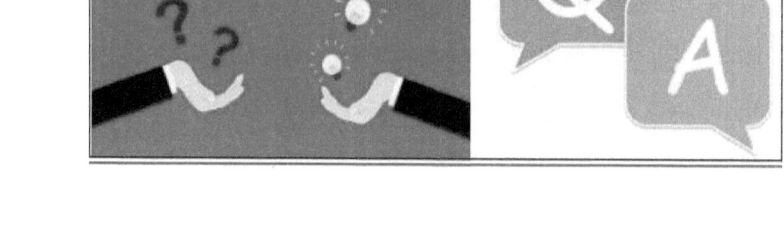

"MBA BASICS IN 24 HOURS!"
Both kindle version & Paperback.
10 Books! Available in Amazon now!

Principles & Practices of Management,
Human Resource Management, Financial Management,
Marketing Management, Organizational Behaviour,
Managerial Economics, Strategic Management & MIS.
+PMP/Proj Management & International Business/Foreign Trade

Search the above title in Amazon

Author: G.R. Narasimhan

ABOUT THE AUTHOR

G.R. Narasimhan – Sr. Consultant for technology and business under **Zodiac Services Chennai** (as on June 2019) which was started in 2010 to serve the people in alternative beliefs/therapies like astrological predictions, prayers, remedies, prasnam (divine words) and vedic guidance for short- or long-term problems, vastu, numerology, gem stones, yantras, mantras or rituals (related areas), yoga, meditation, counseling and alternative therapies consulting. Business & education, soft skills/software/electronics & communication training & promotion, web designing, career counseling and Internet & social media marketing are additionally served. Assisting the entrepreneurship business for the above mentioned areas to serve better for the clients, **G.R. Narasimhan** also the author of few e-books called "A Simple guide to Vedic Astrology," "Inverted Universal Meditation & Engineering," "Secrets of Equity Stocks to make Millions," "Symbolic Meditation & Developing ESP" and many other (are already available in Amazon) having extended experience in IT + Management areas developed website and online marketing using different business strategies and continue the service very well to extend further including this "MBA Basics in 24 Hours with Additional Topics – Global Marketing and Foreign Trade"; – "MBA Basics in 24 Hours with Additional Topics –Management Workbook with Q & A" concepts specifically based on the business administration topics applied overall in the academic/professional curriculum. With the continuous extraordinary ability and skills in research and experience, he is able to explain and train/assist others with extended support and guidance by counseling/consulting effectively.

Great thanks and good luck for everyone reading this book on "MBA Basics in 24 Hours" with almost all the areas of basic business administration or career growth individually or as a group. For any queries and feedback, you can contact directly via email to info@zodiacservices.net, info@astroservices.in or astronara@gmail.com.

CONTENTS

Topic	Page Numbers
Introduction	05
Chapter One - Multiple Choice Questions!	06
Chapter One - Answers : Mutiple Choice Questions	20
Chapter Two - Brief Questions	21
Chapter Two - Answers to Brief Questions	25
Chapter Three - Long Questions	66
Chapter Three - Answers to Long Questions	69
Conclusion	140

"MBA BASICS IN 24 HOURS!"
Both kindle version & Paperback.
10 Books! Available in Amazon now!

Principles & Practices of Management,
Human Resource Management, Financial Management,
Marketing Management, Organizational Behaviour,
Managerial Economics, Strategic Management & MIS.
+PMP/Proj Management & International Business/Foreign Trade

Search the above title in Amazon

Author: G.R. Narasimhan

INTRODUCTION

Business Administration is the combination of different areas of skills in management. Managing and maintaining several departments or areas of activities described in a single umbrella or vertical called management of business administration. The following areas are the main topics or chapters for the discussion under business administration, mostly common for any bachelors or masters studies.

- Principles & Practices of Management
- Human Resource Management
- Financial Management
- Marketing Management
- Organizational Behavior
- Managerial Economics
- Strategic Management
- Management Information Systems

Then there are several branches extended in business administration like foreign trade, global marketing, international business, social work, information technology, project management, six sigma, finance, human resources etc. These eight topics are considered to summarize and define important/ brief summary and keywords under which various chapters for each topic is given (published in Amazon).

This book covers the summaries and definitions as questions & answers suggested "Management Q &A Workbook" with the above mentioned chapters and more!

Some of the chapters given with examples of real time project related terms. But readers must understand the concepts of their own project/ business and other areas. As it has high level of contents in brief which can be covered in few hours/ in a day maximum, readers can read other books from different authors to gain in-depth knowledge of the given business management and administration.

This book gives quick glance & easy go chapters for any situation like interview, short answering, puzzles, examinations and overall explanation to present others. Multiple choices, short and long answer sections are given individually with answers at the end of every chapter. Whoever is preparing for general or specific management interviews or management exams or starting up a firm or organization or training others in the management areas or even conducting test or interviews to others; can have a quick look at the questions and answers to have high level knowledge overall and that leads to answer many questions based on the situation they experience in the real time management projects. **Good Luck!**

Chapter One - Multiple Choice Questions!

Q 1 Management is
   (i) An art
   (ii) A science
   (iii) Both art and science
   (iv) Balance of art and science

Q 2 Managers perform these functions:
   (i) Planning, organising, leading and controlling
   (ii) Planning, organising, developing and controlling
   (iii) Planning, selecting, leading and controlling
   (iv) Planning, organising, leading and correcting

Q 3 Planning involves:
   (i) Setting goals and ways to achieve them
   (ii) Setting of goals and ways to achieve them, and appropriation of resources
   (iii) Setting of goals and ways to achieve them, and organising staff
   (iv) Setting of goals

Q 4 Management is a process of:
   (i) Continuous activities
   (ii) Continuous and overlapping activities
   (iii) Continuous and related activities
   (iv) Continuous and unrelated activities

Q 5 At middle level which is the most important skill the managers should possess?
   (i) Technical skills
   (ii) Human skills
   (iii) Organising skills
   (iv) Conceptual skills

Q 6 In joint venture:
   (i) Two companies come together to achieve common objectives
   (ii) Two companies share profits
   (iii) Two companies merge with each other
   (iv) Two companies come together but don't share profits

Q 7 Which of these is a joint venture:
 (i) Glaxo Smithkline
 (ii) Sony Eriksson
 (iii) HDFC and CBOP
 (iv) P&G and Gillete

Q 8 Babbage was in support of:
 (i) Cost reduction
 (ii) Specialization
 (iii) Wage incentives
 (iv) All of the above

Q 9 Which of these is not a benefit of division of labour?
 (i) Increased specialization
 (ii) Improved efficiency
 (iii) Precision in work
 (iv) Acquisition of new knowledge

Q 10 Soldiering refers to:
 (i) Reduced efficiency
 (ii) Restricting output
 (iii) Restricting labour participation in communication
 (iv) Reduced wages

Q 11 Gantt chart is also known as:
 (i) Daily balance chart
 (ii) Daily work chart
 (iii) Daily activity chart
 (iv) Gantt chart of industrial relations

Q 12 Subordination of individual interest to general interest means:
 (i) Keeping group over individual
 (ii) Keeping management over individual
 (iii) Keeping organization over group or individual
 (iv) Keeping individual over organization

Q 13 Relay assembly test room study shows that:
   (i) Industry has a legal function to perform
   (ii) Industry has a leadership function to perform
   (iii) Industry has social function to perform
   (iv) Industry has intellectual function to perform

Q 14 Group collaboration occurs by:
   (i) Accident
   (ii) Planning and development
   (iii) Individual interests
   (iv) Force of management

Q 15 Non-economic reward doesn't include:
   (i) Bonus
   (ii) Sense of belongingness
   (iii) Recognition
   (iv) Felicitation

Q 16 Calculative involvement is:
   (i) One where employee is mentally absent from work
   (ii) One where employee is just concerned with the job
   (iii) One where the employee is personally involved
   (iv) One where employee is not personally involved

Q 17 Which of these is not an example of environmental changes,
   (i) Change in consumer preferences
   (ii) Change in policies of government
   (iii) Change in production techniques
   (iv) Change in demand

Q18 While doing diagnosis the study of which relationship is not important,
   (i) Between people peers
   (ii) Between boss subordinate
   (iii) Between units doing different tasks
   (iv) Between people and informal systems

Q 19 Which of these is not as important as others to improve employee-organization relations,
- (i) Rewards
- (ii) Equity
- (iii) Fair trade practices
- (iv) Leadership

Q 20 In a dynamic environment with high complexity,
- (i) Considerable leadership but little management is required
- (ii) Little leadership but considerable management is required
- (iii) Considerable leadership and management is required
- (iv) Little management and leadership is required

Q 21 Culture in its broadest sense is:
- (i) Behavior
- (ii) Cultivated behavior
- (iii) Organizational behavior
- (iv) Ethical behavior

Q 22 Which of these show variation in culture?
- (i) Difference in wage system in 2 organizations
- (ii) Difference in work hours of 2 organizations
- (iii) Difference in structure of 2 organizations
- (iv) All of the above

Q 23 Which of these is not a material culture?
- (i) Clothes
- (ii) Clothes designed for lawyers
- (iii) Technology
- (iv) Compulsion that traffic policemen should be in white dress

Q 24 A standard way of working in an organization refers to its:
- (i) Norms
- (ii) Values
- (iii) Beliefs
- (iv) Philosophy

Q 25 Try if you like it' means
   (i) People are forced to accept change
   (ii) People are given rewards to accept change
   (iii) People are given time to experience the change
   (iv) People don't accept the change

Q 26 Conflict between administrative action and cultural values in an organization can be sorted out by:
   (i) Accepting existing culture
   (ii) Making alterations in culture
   (iii) Motivating employees to acept administrative actions
   (iv) Threatening employees to accept administrative actions

Q 27 Data processing doesn't include one of these steps:
   (i) Comparison
   (ii) Classification
   (iii) Analysis
   (iv) Correction

Q 28 Information can be used to:
   (i) Make decisions
   (ii) Maximizing revenues
   (iii) Minimizing costs
   (iv) All of the above

Q 29 Marketing department is getting information on raw materials purchased. This is an issue of:
   (i) Quality
   (ii) Relevance
   (iii) Quantity
   (iv) Timeliness

Q 30 _____ enables users to contact remote computers and interact with them.
   (i) E-mail
   (ii) File Transfer Protocol
   (iii) Telnet
   (iv) Web

Q 31 Which one of these not an essential for extranet?
   (i) Intranet
   (ii) Internet
   (iii) Firewall
   (iv) Group-ware applications

Q 32 Which of these is not a form of DSS software?
   (i) Excel
   (ii) Lotus
   (iii) PowerPoint
   (iv) Quatro

Q 33 A manger takes decision regarding change in rewards structure. It is a _____ decision.
   (i) Intuitive
   (ii) Policy
   (iii) Operating
   (iv) Programmed

Q 34 The most important stage in decision making process is,
   (i) identification of the problems
   (ii) evaluating alternatives
   (iii) selecting alternatives
   (iv) implementation

Q 35 Importance of decisions is that:
   (i) they are strategic
   (ii) they are long term
   (iii) they are time consuming
   (iv) they result in profit

Q 36 Which of these is not true in context of group decision-making?
   (i) they result in well balanced decisions
   (ii) they facilitate creativity
   (iii) they are more cost effective
   (iv) they increase commitment

Q37 In_____ situation, manager has unreliable and little information.
   (i) Certainty
   (ii) Risk
   (iii) Uncertainty
   (iv) Low-risk

Q 38 Delphi Technique was developed by:
   (i) Procter & Gamble
   (ii) Delphi Corporation
   (iii) Rand Corporation
   (iv) General Motors

Q 39 In _____, all the ideas are enlisted and evaluated.
   (i) Brainstorming
   (ii) Garden Technique
   (iii) Nominal Group Technique
   (iv) Attribute Listing

Q 40 The demand for a commodity is said to be elastic if the total amount spent on it is
   (i) Less when the price is low than when the price is high.
   (ii) More when the price is low than when the price is high.
   (iii) The same whether the price is high or low.

Q 41 Elasticity is
   (i) The slope of demand curve
   (ii) Usually greater than unity
   (iii) Usually less than unity
   (iv) A ratio of relative changes between a dependent and an independent variable.

Q 42 If demand is inelastic and price increase:
   (i) Total revenue will fall
   (ii) Total revenue will rise
   (iii) Total revenue will be unchanged.

Q 43 An isoquant is:
   (i) The least-cost combination.
   (ii) A locus of input combinations that gives rise to the same level of output, provided the firm is minimizing production cost.
   (iii) A locus of input combinations of factor-inputs that the firm can buy with a given outlay and factor prices.

Q 44 The law of diminishing return states that:
   (i) The returns on stocks and bonds diminish with higher security prices.
   (ii) Beyond some point, the increment or addition to total utility diminishes as more units of a good are consumed.
   (iii) The marginal physical product of any factor of production will eventually diminish as more of that factor is used with a given amount of fixed input.
   (iv) The output of any good or service increases as more variable input is used.

Q 45 Marginal cost curve cuts the average cost curve:
   (i) At the left of its lowest point.
   (ii) At its lowest point.
   (iii) At the right of its lowest paint.

Q 46 Economies of scale:
   (i) Exist in both short-run and the long-run.
   (ii) Explain why average variable and average total costs decline in the short-run.
   (iii) Explain why average costs decline for a given rate of   output in the long-run.
   (iv) Explain why average costs increase for a given rate of output in the long-run.

Q 47 Diseconomies of scale are reflected in:
   (i) The rising segment of the long-run average cost curve.
   (ii) The rising segment of the short-run marginal cost curve.
   (iii) Greater efficiency that results from specialization.
   (iv) Downward shifts of the production cost curves.

Q 48 The U-shapedness of the long-run average cost curve reflects:
   (i) The law of variable proportions.
   (ii) The technological changes.
   (iii) The laws of returns to scale.
   (iv) None of these.

Q 49 The statement of an organization's commitment to quality is a
   (i) Policy
   (ii) Vision
   (iii) Mission
   (iv) Principle
   (v) Goal

Q 50 Which of the following is not a defect metric?
   (i) Location
   (ii) Cause
   (iii) Time to fix
   (iv) Classification
   (v) Coverage
   (vi) All of the above

Q 51 The basis upon which adherence to policies is measured is
   (i) Standard
   (ii) Requirement
   (iii) Expected result
   (iv) Value
   (v) All of the above
   (vi) None of the above

Q 52 Which of the following does not form a part of a workbench?
   (i) Standards
   (ii) Quality attributes
   (iii) Quality control
   (iv) Procedures
   (v) Rework

Q 53 The focus on the product is highest during
   (i) a walkthrough
   (ii) a checkpoint review
   (iii) an inspection

O 54 The Quality manager will find it difficult to effectively implement the QAI Quality Improvement Process, unless his organization is willing to accept the Quality principles as
   (i) The organization's policy
   (ii) A challenge
   (iii) The corporate vision
   (iv) The organization's goal
   (v) A management philosophy
   (vi) All of the above

Q 55 Baselines measure the _____ change.
   (i) Situation prior to
   (ii) Expectation of benefits of
   (iii) Effects of
   (iv) Desirability of
   (v) None of the above

Q 56 Modifying existing standards to better match the need of a project or environment is
   (i) Definition
   (ii) Standard for a standard
   (iii) Tailoring
   (iv) Customization
   (v) None of the above

Q 57 Malcolm Baldridge National Quality Award has the following eligibility categories/ dimensions
   (i) Approach
   (ii) Deployment
   (iii) Results
   (iv) All of the above
   (v) Manufacturing, Service and small businesses
   (vi) None of the above

Q 58 The term "benchmarking" means
   (i) Comparing with past data from your organization
   (ii) Comparing with the results of a market survey
   (iii) Comparing with the results of a customer survey
   (iv) None of the above

Q 59 An example of deployment of a quality approach is:
   (i) The degree to which the approach embodies effective evaluation cycles
   (ii) The appropriate and effective application to all product and service characteristics
   (iii) The effectiveness of the use of tools, techniques, and methods
   (iv) The contribution of outcomes and effects to quality improvement
   (v) The significance of improvement to the company's business

Q 60 The activity which includes confirming understanding, brainstorming and testing ideas is a
   (i) Code walkthrough
   (ii) Inspection
   (iii) Review
   (iv) Structured walkthrough

Q 61 The following can be considered to measure quality:
   (i) Customer satisfaction
   (ii) Defects
   (iii) Rework
   (iv) All of the above
   (v) None of the above

Q 62 The most common reason for the presence of a large number of bugs in a software product is,
   (i) Incompetence of the developer
   (ii) Incompetence of the tester
   (iii) Bad requirements
   (iv) Wrong use of tools and techniques

Q 63 The objective of TQM is
- (i) To improve processes
- (ii) To improve profitability
- (iii) All of the above
- (iv) None of the above

Q 64 System Test Plan will not include
- (i) Approach
- (ii) Pass/Fail criteria
- (iii) Risks
- (iv) Suspension and Resumption criteria
- (v) None of the above

Q 65 The following is NOT a category in MBNQA criteria:
- (i) Leadership
- (ii) HR Focus
- (iii) Quality Management
- (iv) Information and Analysis
- (v) None of the above

Q 66 Complaints must be resolved within
- (i) An hour
- (ii) Four minutes
- (iii) A day
- (iv) Four hours
- (v) None of the above

Q 67 The purpose of cost-of -quality computations is to show how much is being spent for the quality control and quality assurance program.
- (i) True
- (ii) False

Q 68 The method by which release from the requirements of a specific standard may be obtained for a specific situation is a
   (i) Tailoring
   (ii) Customization
   (iii) Force Field Analysis
   (iv) Waiver
   (v) None of the above

Q 69 Measures designed to minimize the probability of modification, destruction, or inability to retrieve software or data is
   (i) Preventive security
   (ii) Corrective security
   (iii) Protective security
   (iv) None of the above

Q 70 Quality assurance is a function responsible for
   (i) Controlling quality
   (ii) Managing quality
   (iii) Inspections
   (iv) Removal of defects

Q 71 Statistical methods are used to differentiate random variation from
   (i) Standards
   (ii) Assignable variation
   (iii) Control limits
   (iv) Specification limits

Q 72 An increase in cash reserve ratio will cause yield curve to
   (i) Shift downward
   (ii) Remain unchanged
   (iii) Become steeper
   (iv) Become flatter

Q 73 A bank holds a securty that is rated A+. The rating of the security migrates to A. What is the risk that the bank has faced?
   (i) Market risk
   (ii) Operational risk
   (iii) Market liquidation risk
   (iv) Credit risk

Q 74 When interest rates go up. prices of fixed interest bonds.....
   (i) Go up
   (ii) Go down
   (iii) Remain unchanged

Q 75 VaR is not enough to assess market risk of a portfolio. Stress testing is desirable because
   (i) It helps in calibrating VaR module
   (ii) It helps as an additional risk measure
   (iii) It helps in assessing risk due to abnormal movement of market parameters
   (iv) It is used as VaR measure is not accurate enough

Q 76 When the interest rates fall, the market price of a fixed rate bond
   (i) falls
   (ii) rises
   (iii) does not change

Q 77 A transaction where financial securities are issued against the cash flow generated from a pool of assets is called
   (i) Securitization
   (ii) Credit Default Swaps
   (iii) Credit Linked Notes
   (iv) Total Return Swaps

Q 78 12% Government of India security is quoted at Rs.120. If interest rates go down by 1%, the market price of the security will be
   (i) Rs. 120
   (ii) Rs.133.3
   (iii) Rs. 109
   (iv) Rs. 140

Q 79 A fall in long term interest rates on Government securities will make the yield curve become
  (i) flatter
  (ii) steeper
  (iii) shift downward

Q 80 Back testing is done to
  (i) Test a model
  (ii) Compare model results and actual performance
  (iii) Record performance
  (iv) None of the above

Chapter One - Answers : Mutiple Choice Questions

1. (iv)	2. (i)	3. (ii)	4. (ii)	5. (iv)
6. (i)	7. (ii)	8. (iv)	9. (iv)	10. (ii)
11. (i)	12. (iii)	13. (iii)	14. (ii)	15. (i)
16. (ii)	17. (iii)	18. (iv)	19. (iii)	20. (iii)
21. (ii)	22. (iv)	23. (iv)	24. (i)	25. (iii)
26. (i)	27. (iv)	28. (iv)	29. (ii)	30. (iii)
31. (i)	32. (iii)	33. (ii)	34. (iv)	35. (i)
36. (iii)	37. (ii)	38. (iii)	39. (iv)	40. (i)
41. (iv)	42. (ii)	43. (iii)	44. (iii)	45. (ii)
46. (iii)	47. (i)	48. (iii)	49. (i)	50. (vi)
51. (i)	52. (ii)	53. (ii)	54. (vi)	55. (i)
56. (iii)	57. (v)	58. (iv)	59. (iii)	60. (iii)
61. (iv)	62. (iv)	63. (i)	64. (iii)	65. (iii)
66. (ii)	67. (ii)	68. (iv)	69. (i)	70. (ii)
71. (iii)	72. (iv)	73. (iv)	74. (ii)	75. (iii)
76. (ii)	77. (i)	78. (ii)	79. (i)	80. (ii)

Chapter Two - Brief Questions

Q1 What is marketing? List few of the terms associated with marketing.

Q 2 What are the bases of marketing?

Q 3 What is Sales?

Q 4 What is the scope of marketing?

Q 5 What are the objectives of marketing?

Q 6 What are the elements of scientific management.

Q 7 What are the different variables used for segmentation?

Q 8 Define: (1) Depth segmentation (2) Cluster analysis

Q 9 What is meant by the by-product of market segmentation? Give example.

Q 10 What are the various considerations for market segmentation?

Q 11 What are the various steps involved in product positioning in the selected market segment?

Q 12 What is Rational Document meant for?

Q 13 What are the inclusions of rational document?

Q 14 "A message strategy is a time saver". Comment.

Q 15 What is the positioning of : a) Nano car from Tata b) Airtel-DTH service.

Q 16 How and why the concept of product life cycle is used as a tool for market development? Write its benefits.

Q 17 Explain the major objectives of advertising and publicity with suitable examples.

Q 18 Distinguish primary data from secondary data. What are the merits, demerits and limitations?

Q 19 Describe the five important functions performed by Production/Operational manager.

Q 20 Define job design

Q 21 Define job analysis.

Q 22 How can job design help with the organization of work?

Q 23 What are features of "good" job design?

Q 24 What are common approaches to job design?

Q 25 What are the overall goals of job design?

Q 26 what are the elements of functional information systems?

Q 27 What is the objectives of the management in using MIS?

Q 28 What are the functions of MIS in management?

Q 29 What are the expectations of the management of MIS?

Q 30 What are the factors on which success/failure of MIS depends?

Q 31 A small accounting firm pays each of its five clerks Rs 25000, two junior accountants Rs 60000, and the firm's owner Rs 255000. What is the mean salary paid at the firm? How many of the employees earn less than the mean? What is the median salary?

Q 32 Nonstandard dice can produce interesting distributions of outcomes. You have two balanced, six-sided dice. One is a standard dice, with faces having 1,2,3,4,5 and 6 spots. The other dice has three faces with 0 spots and three faces with 6 spots. Find the probability distribution for the total number of spots Y on the up-faces when you roll these two dice.

Q 33 A study of iron deficiency among infants compared samples of infants following different feeding regimens. One group contained breast-fed infants. While the children in other group were fed a standard baby formula without any iron supplements. Here are summary results on blood hemoglobin levels at 12 months of age.

Q 34 What do you mean by a seasonal index? Explain ration to link relatives method of measuring seasonal variations.

Q 35 Briefly explain the 7s model.

Q 36 State 7S Checklist Questions.

Q 37 Take two examples of the political changes in the country. Explain how these changes have lead to the changes in the business environment.

Q 38 Write short notes on: Retrenchment strategy

Q 39 Write short notes on: Concentric diversification.

Q 40 What is the significance of Boston Consulting Group Box ("BCG Box")?

Q 41 What are the contributions of Scientific Management?

Q 42 Why is organization development important?

Q 43 Describe the recruitment policy of any organization.

Q 44 What are the benefits of HR resourcing?

Q 45 Discuss the meaning and objectives of performance appraisal.

Q 46 Explain the methods of collecting information for job analysis in your organization or any organization you are familiar with. Describe the organization you are referring to.

Q 47 Why human resource planning is important? Describe the forecasting techniques that are being used for human resource planning in your organization or any organization you are acquainted with. Describe the organization you are referring to.

Q 48 What is knowledge management?

Q 49 Why do we need to manage knowledge?

Q 50 What are the boundaries?

Q 51 What is a boundaryless organization?

Q 52 Can an organization be completely boundaryless?

Q 53 What makes a virtual organization different?

Q 54 Discuss the strategies adopted for organizational restructuring in an organization.

Q 55 What are the Basic Characteristics of Organizational Structure?

Q 56 What is Human Relations Approach?

Q 57 What is Job Characteristics Approach?

Q 58 What is meant by-Work Breaks/Rest Breaks?

Q 59 What are the main features of an MIS?

Q 60 Explain the term technology with reference to Modern Age?

Chapter Two - Answers to Brief Questions

Ans. 1.

It is a process by which

one identifies the needs and wants of the people.

one determines and creates a product/service to meet the needs and wants.

one determines a way of taking the product/service to the market place.

one determines the way of communicating the product to the market place.

one determines the value for the product.

one determines the people, who have needs/ wants.

creating a transaction for exchanging the product for a value, and thus creating a satisiaction to the buyer's needs/wants.

Terms to understand.

1. Product/Service means a product or service or idea to satisty the people's needs/wants.
2. Needs mean when a person feels deprived of something.
3. Wants mean when a person's need is formed/shaped by personality, culture, and knowledge.
4. Value means the benefits that the customer gains from owning and using the product and the cost of the product.
5. Satisfaction means the extent to which a product's perceived performance matches a buyer's expectation.
6. Exchange means the act of obtaining a needed/ wanted object by offering something in return.

Transactions mean a trade off between a buyer/a seller that involves an exchange at agreed conditions.

Ans. 2.

Marketing is based on identifying, anticipating and satisfying customer needs effectively and profitably. It encompasses
- market research,
- product planning/development,
- product pricing, -product marketing
- sales and promotion,
- distribution,
- customer care,
- branding
- merchandising
- retailing
- website marketing and much more.

From the above, we conclude "sales" is one of the elenents of total marketing.

Ans. 3.

It is a process by which -one identifies the people, who have a need. [Prospecting]
- one determines the needs of the people.
- one determines a way of finding a solution to the prospect's problem.
- one determines the way of communicating your product as a solution.
- one determines the value for the product for the prospect.
- one determines/sells benefits of the product to the prospect. and then creating a transaction for exchanging the product for a value and thus creating a satisfaction to the buyer's needs/wants.

Ans 4.

Establish, direct, administer and coordinate the overall product marketing programs for all Products. Strategically plan for, develop and profitably penetrate the markets to which the products, services and capabilities of the company can be directed. These activities include –studying economic indicators –tracking changes in supply and demand – identifying customers and their current and future needs –monitoring the competition.

Ans 5

Prime objective of marketing is:
- to support and help the organization to achieve the Corporate

The second important objective of marketing is:
- to enable the organization survive and prosper through meeting needs and wants of customers by matching a company's capabilities with customer needs/wants.

Third objective is:
- to provide an agreed. Consistent and well directed target range of volume for all departmental functions, which will help them to streamline their activities for the period.
    - ❖ finance
    - ❖ manufacturing/ production
    - ❖ human resource etc.

Fourth objective is:
- to provide the marketing department a tool to plan and manage its activities,

Fifth objective is:
- To provide a stretch points for setting sub-objectives /planning/ strategies for marketing department.
    - ❖ market share target.
    - ❖ competitive standing target.
    - ❖ customer awareness target.
    - ❖ customer retention target.
    - ❖ new products target

Sixth objective is:
- to provide a method devised to achieve the objectives in the promotion Mix.

Seventh objective is:
- to provide a stretch points for setting sub-objectives /planning/ strategies for Sales Management.
    - ❖ product coverage.
    - ❖ customer coverage.
    - ❖ geographical area coverage. etc

Eighth objective is:
- to provide a stretch points for setting sub-objectives /planning/ strategies for Distributon Managenent.
    - ❖ distribution penetration target.

Ninth objective is:
- to provide a stretch points for setting sub-objectives /planning/ strategies for Customer Service Management
  - ❖ customer satisfaction level.

Tenth objective is:
- to provide a stretch points for setting sub-objectives/planning/strategies for Overall Control through Research
  - ❖ consumer research.
  - ❖ customer satisfaction surveys.
  - ❖ internal operation research.
  - ❖ distribution study
  - ❖ marketing research etc

Ans. 6.
Elements:
- Labor is defined and authority/responsibility is legitimised/official
- Positions placed in hierarchy and under authority of higher level
- Selection is based upon technical competence, training or experience
- Actions and decisions are recorded to allow continuity and memory
- Management is different from ownership of the organization
- Managers follow rules/procedures to enable reliable/predictable behavior

Ans. 7.

The variables used for segmentation include:

1. Geographic variables
   - region of the world or country, East, West, South, North, Central, coastal, hilly, etc.
   - country size/country size : Metropolitian Cities, small cities, towns.
   - Density of Area Urban, Semi-urban, Rural.
   - climate Hot, Cold, Humid, Rainy.
2. Demographic variables
   - age
   - gender Male and Female
   - sexual orientation
   - family size
   - family life cycle
   - Education Primary, High School, Secondary, College, Universities.
   - income
   - occupation
   - education
3. Socioeconomic status
   - religion
   - nationality/race
   - language
4. Psychographic variables
   - personality
   - life style
   - value
   - attitude
5. Behavioural variables
   - benefit sought
   - product usage rate
   - brand loyalty
   - product end use
   - readiness-to-buy stage
   - decision making unit
   - profitability

Ans 8
When numerous variables are combined to give an in-depth understanding of a segment, this is reletred to as depth Segmentation.

When enough information is combined to create a clear picture of a typical member of a segment, this is referred to as a buyer profile. When the profile is limited to demographic variables it is called a demographic profile (typically shortened to "a demographic "). A statistical technique commonly used in determining a profile is cluster analysis.

Ans. 9.
The by-product of market segmentation is the identification of the particular segment, larget market which one wants to exploit.
Nano " small car" in universal term, the nano is a small car.
In Indian Term
- nano is specifically designed for the Indian market
- it is designed for the Indian market -it is designed "as a value for money"
- it is designed with India made parts.

Ans. 10.
The Market Segmentation Variables Considered
For the Businesses
- reduction in capital expenses
- reduction in operation expenses
- reduction in maintenance expenses.
- improvement in the cash flow.
- improvement in the working conditions for field employees
- improvement in the productivity of field employees. -improvement in the business market coverage
- improvement in the business results.

For the Individuals
1. Demographic variables
    - age
    - gender Male and Female
    - sexual orientation
    - family size
    - family life cycle
    - Education Primary, High School, Secondary, College, Universities.
    - income
    - occupation
    - education
2. Socioeconomic status
    - religion
    - Regional Focus
    - language
3. Geographic variables
    - region of the country, North/South/ East/ West/Central etc.
    - metro/ rural : Metropolitan Cities, small cities, towns.
    - Density of Area Urban, Semi-urban, Rural.
    - climate Hot, Cold, Humid, Rainy.
4. Psychographic variables
    - personality
    - life style
    - value
    - attitude
5. Behavioural variables
    - benefit sought
    - product usage rate
    - brand loyalty
    - product end use
    - readiness-to-buy stage
    - decision making unit
    - profitability
    - income status

Ans. 11.
The first step in the positioning process is to do the research. The good news is that product marketing managers
already have done most of the research as part of their job. To successfully position a product, you need a thorough
understanding of customer problems, channel issues, and how competitors are positioned. The answers to these and
other questions become part of a rationale document for your positioning strategy:

- What is your target market (size, type of company, etc.)?
- Who is the decision maker you want to target your message to, and what keeps that decision maker awake at
- night?
- What pressing problem does your product solve for your prospective customer?
- How is your prospect solving that problem today? What specific benefit does your product deliver?
- Why is your product better than the current solution and competitive alternatives?
- Who are your key competitors; why and when do you win or lose to them?
- How do your competitors position themselves in their marketing communications, including ads, direct mail campaigns, brochures, and web sites?
- What makes your product unique in a way that is relevant to your prospect?
- Are there any problems, unique challenges, or special needs of your channel? What do prospects and customers like and dislike about your product?
- Do prospects and customers share your belief of why your product is better than the competition's?
- Are there any characteristics of a sales situation that indicate whether or not your product or service will be selected?

Now incorporate the answers to these questions in a rationale document. By doing so, all product knowledge is captured in one place and can be used as a reference guide when marketing and sales need it.

Ans. 12.

A Rationale Document Captures All the Praduct Knowledge In addition to documenting product knowledge, the positioning process improves marketing without intense, time-consuming input from product marketing. A message strategy is like the recipe for how to talk about your poduct. Follow the recipe rather than ask product marketing, and your marketers can create a compelling, accurate story about your product.

This does not mean that your product marketing managers no longer need to be involved in the planning and creation of marketing materials. They should provide input when appropriate. It's just that the process won't take up nearly as much of their time. That's because marketing gets most of its infusion of product knowledge by referencing the rationale document and message strategy. And that means your product marketing managers have successfully cloned themselves; they'll have more time for other competing priorities.

Ans. 13.

The rationale document should be three to five pages and should include following information:

Product Category: Define the product's key features, advantages, and benefits. A matrix can help clarify these items.

Product Line Fit: Describe how the product fits into the overall company product strategy.

Situation Analysis: Describe the conditions that justify the release of this product, including why the company
believes it can be successful.

Market Analysis: Profile target market(s) by size, revenue, market segment, operational type, or other relevant categories.

Audience Analysis: Profile key prospects within the target market(s), including job titles and functions (demographics)
and their concerns, attitudes, and behaviors (psychographics)

Distribution: Describe how the product will be distributed and the impact of distribution on product communications.

Competitive Positioning: Describe the key competitors, their targets, and how they position their products.

Positioning Statement and Rationale: Evaluate the product positioning statement against the following four criteria:
Is it important unique, believable, and usable?

Support Points: Describe how the three support points make the positioning statement unique, believable, and important. If multiple markets or audiences require unique support points, explain why.

Ans. 14.

Your positioning statement becomes the central idea and theme underlying all marketing activities. It is a short,
compelling, declarative sentence that states just one benefit and addresses the target market's number one problem.
it must be unique, believable, and important, or the target market will ignore the message. Once you have found the
right message, your product marketing managers won't need to be involved in every planning session for every marketing campaign.
Supporting benefit statements tell the story in more detail. They also provide a structure for product demonstrations.
While the positioning statement articulates a high-level benefit, the claims made in the supporting statements should be readily demonstrable. That is, in just a few steps, you should be able to show how the product delivers concrete benefits. Make sure your message strategy has enough detail to support the creation of a standard product demonstration. This helps your product marketing managers to create a demo quickly. And there's another benefit-the product detail in the support points answers a lot questions before marketing and sales ask them.

A message strategy also facilitates delivery of the same message across all marketing media, including web sites, brochures, advertisements, and presentations to investors, industry analysts, and prospects. A standard outline format makes it easy for writers and other communicators to see the message strategy's benefit hierarchy, and to take full advantage of it.

Ans.15.

1. Nano
    - ❖ segment-middle class.
    - ❖ Target---upper income brack [400,000 --1million rupees]
    - ❖ Positioning ----affordable/Convenient
2. AIRTEL-DTH
    - ❖ Segment-middle class
    - ❖ Target Families with median income.
    - ❖ Positioning- entertainment for all situations.

Ans. 16.

Product Life Cycle

Products pass through a series of stages. Successful products progress through four basic stages: (1) Introduction (2) Growth; (3) Maturity; and (4) Decline.

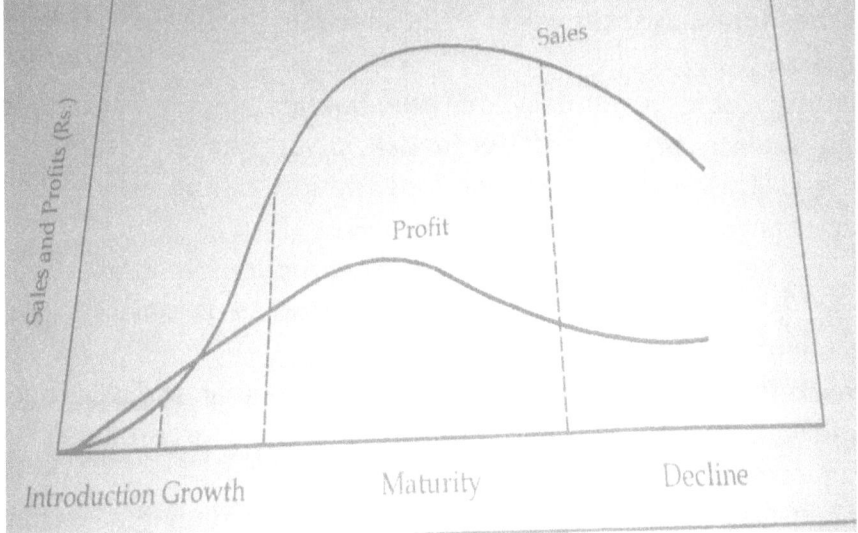

The product life cycle concept provides important insights about developments at the various stages of the product's life. Knowledge that profits assume a predictable pattern through the stages and the promotional emphasis should shift from product information in the early stages to product promotion in the later stages should allow the marketing manager to improve planning.

Product Life Cycle Benefits

Here is a brief description of what is expected to take place in the stages of the life cycle:

1. Initiation starts with the initial conception or discovery of the product idea and runs until it has been evaluated, has become specific, and has been approved for development.

2. Development covers the various activities that transform an abstract product idea into a concrete prototype model of the product (if it is a tangible good) that can be manufactured.

3. Market plans and tests is our term for the final gestation phase, in which the product would pass its last tests and everything be ready for commercialising it.

4. Introduction starts when the offering is made available to buyers, probably on a limited scale, and continues as it is tried by innovators and experiences show slow sales growth

5. Growth begins when numerous tryers like the product, word of its virtues spread, and the product sales "take off". Since the product is not established until this takes place, we include it in this chapter of "evolving products.

6. Maturity comes eventually, for the halcyon days of sharply rising demand vanish when most potential buyers have become actual customers. This may be a very long period during which demand decelerates and then reaches a plateau.

7. Decline sets in persistently when the product eventually becomes obsolete. When it actually starts to toboggan, it is time to give the product a merciful death and burial.

The marketing strategist should never assume that the PLC operates inexorably, but should rather examine a brand's or product's actual position carefully. Further a serious effort should be made to find a winning strategy can revive a slumping demand, rather than summarily abandoning the possibiility. In that context, the PLC does pose a hypothesis of product or brand behaviour that is useful for sales forecasting. It also enables us to clarify strategies in terms of their timeliness.

Ans.17.

The Major Objectives
- Goals that an organization seeks to achieve through its promotional program in terms of communication effects such as
- creating awareness of the product/brand,
- knowledge of the product/brand[features/benefits of the product usage]
- images of the product/brand,
- attitudes of the users of the product,
- help people to show their preferences for the product,
- help people to make the purchase intentions.
- Increasing response rates
- Contributing to ROI business goals, Build a brand image

- Test customer awareness of brand recognition and perceived values Increase Sales
- Levels of repeat purchase Build customer loyalty and relationship
- Levels of customer retention Change customer attitudes
- Measure demographic profile of purchases
- Measure type of goods ordered by new purchasers.
- Compare with previous data. Stimulate an increase in sales
- Number of enquiries from advert,
- Number of enquiries converted into sales Remind customers of the existence of a product
- Text customer awareness both before and after the advertising campaign,
- Number of enquiries Inform customers
- Test customer awareness,
- Number of requests for further information

Objectives could Include
- creates product awareness
- makes known product availability
- creates product perception
- helps to develop product memory
- helps to develop a brand image
- creates a desire
- develops a want
- stirs up the brand
- harnesses the desire
- helps in making the buying decision
- helps to influence the choice
- helps in buying

The Classic Example of Advertising/ Policy Objectives is the "Lux" Toilet Soap [Well Known Branded Product]

1 Awareness
- ❖ many people are aware of the product.
- ❖ many people know what the product is.
- ❖ many people are aware of the brand.

2 Comprehension
- ❖ people understand what the product does.
- ❖ people know the benefits of using it.
- ❖ people can differentiate from other such brands.

3 Conviction
- ❖ people are convinced about the benefits.
- ❖ people who use it can feel the benefits.
- ❖ people enjoy the fuzzy feeling/goodness of the lux.

4 Action
- ❖ people are buying
- ❖ there is repeat purchase.

"MBA BASICS IN 24 HOURS!"
Both kindle version & Paperback.
10 Books! Available in Amazon now!

Principles & Practices of Management,
Human Resource Management, Financial Management,
Marketing Management, Organizational Behaviour,
Managerial Economics, Strategic Management & MIS.
+PMP/Proj Management & International Business/Foreign Trade

Search the above title in Amazon

Author: G R Narasimhan

Ans. 18.

1. Primary Research

Primary Sources

Definitions of primary sources:

Primary sources are original materials on which other research is based They are usually the first formal appearance of results in the print or electronic literature (for example, the first publication of the results of scientific investigations is a primary source.) They present information in its original form, neither interpreted nor condensed nor evaluated by other writers.

They are from the time period (for example, something written close to when what it is recording happened is likely to be a primary source.)

Primary sources present original thinking, report on discoveries, or share new information.

Examples of primary sources:

scientific journal articles reporting experimental research results proceedings of Meetings, Conferences and Symposia. Technical reports dissertations or theses (may also be secondary) patents sets of data, such as census statistics works of literature (such as poems and fiction) diaries autobiographies interviews, surveys and fieldwork letters and correspondence speeches newspaper articles (may also be secondary) government documents photographs and works of art original documents (such as birth certificate or trial transcripts) Internet communications on email, listservs, and newsgroups.

ALSO

means gathering information directly from the consumers which could involve

- using questionnaire.
- using focus group[face to face interview]
- telephone interviews
- panel interviews
- person to person interviews etc

1. Merits
    ❖ from the primary source.
    ❖ original information.
    ❖ current data.
    ❖ reliable.
    ❖ clearly defined.

2. Demerits
- ❖ Time consuming.
- ❖ expensive process.
- ❖ difficult to procure, sometimes.

3. Limitations
- ❖ due to time/cost factors, the amount of data gathering is restricted.

2 Secondary Research

Secondary Sources

Secondary sources are less easily defined than primary sources. What some define as a secondary source, others define as a tertiary source. Nor is it always easy to distinguish primary from secondary sources. A newspaper article is a primary source if it reports events, but a secondary source if it analyses and comments on those events. In science, secondary sources are those which simplify the process of finding and evaluating the primary literature. They tend to be works which repackage, reorganize, reinterpret, summarise, index or otherwise "add value" to the new information reported in the primary literature. More generally, secondary sources

Definitions of Secondary Sources:

Describe, interpret, analyze and evaluate the primary sources comment on and discuss the evidence provided by primary sources are works which are one or more steps removed from the event or information they refer to, being written after the fact with the benefit of hindsight.

Examples of secondary sources:

bibliographies (may also be teritary) biographical works commentaries dictionaries and encylopedias (may also be teritary) dissertations or theses (more usually primary) handbooks and data compilations (may also be teritary) history indexing and abstracting tools used to locate primary & secondary sources(may also be teritary) journal articles, particularly in disciplines other than science(may also be primary) monographs (other than fiction and autobiography) newspaper and popular magazine articles (may also be primary) review articles and literature reviews textbooks (may also be teritary) treatises works of criticism and interpretation ALSO means gathering information indirectly from the published source which could involve –using census data. – buying published data from bureaus –gathering data from stock exchange –collecting information from campany annual reports, etc

1. Merits
   - ❖ from the secondary source
   - ❖ easy to source
   - ❖ less time required.
   - ❖ less expensive.
2. Demerits
   - ❖ repackaged information.
   - ❖ re-interpretation.
   - ❖ not so reliable.
   - ❖ old data and not current.
3. Limitations.
   - ❖ not current data.

Ans.19.
The Five Key Functions of Production/Operation Manager:
1. With the Planning & Production Manager, develop, direct the implementation of production business strategies and activities to enable the production to achieve output and quality objectives.
2. Manage and Control the logistics function to ensure supplies of raw materials, finished goods, parts and accessories are available within required time frames and budgets.
3. With the R&D Engineering Manager, develop, direct the the research & development/ engineering activities to ensure products and techniques achieve business needs within the standards set by the market and the regulatory standards bodies.
4. With the Warehouse and Distribution Manager, develop, direct and control the warehouse and distribubon activities to ensure the efficient and economical utilization of facilities for storing and distributing the finished goods.
5. With the Manufacturing Services Manager, develop, direct the implementation of manufacturing sustainability strategies/ actions plans and continuous improvement programs.

Ans. 20.
Job design refers to the way that a set of tasks, or an entire job, is organized. Job design helps to determine
- what tasks are done,
- how the tasks are done,
- how many tasks are done, and
- in what order the tasks are done.

It takes into account all factors which affect the work, and organizes the content and tasks so that the whole job is less likely to be a risk to the employee. Job design involves administrative areas such as:
- job rotation,
- job enlargement,
- task/machine pacing.
- work breaks,
- and working hours.

A well designed job will encourage a variety of 'good' body positions, have reasonable strength requirements, require a reasonable amount of mental activity, and help foster feelings of achievement and self-esteem.

Ans. 21.
Job Analysis is a process to identify and determine in detail the particular job duties and requirements and the relative importance of these duties lor a given job. Job Analysis is a process where judgements are made about data collected on a job. The Job; not the person An important concept of Job Analysis is that the analysis is conducted of the Job, not the person. While Job Analysis data may be collected from incumbents through interviews or questionnaires, the product of the analysis is a description or specifications of the job, not a description of the person. Purpose of Job Analysis The purpose of Job Analysis is to establish and document the 'job relatedness' of employment procedures such as training, selection, compensation, and performance appraisal.

Ans. 22.
Job design principles can address problems such as: work overload, work underload, repetitiveness, limited control over work, isolation, shiftwork, delays in filling vacant positions, excessive working hours, and limited understanding of the whole job process. Job design is sometimes considered as a way to help deal with stress in the workplace.

Ans. 23.

Good job design accommodates employees' mental and physical characteristics by paying attention to: muscular energy such as work/rest schedules or pace of work, and mental energy such as boring versus extremely difficult tasks. Good job design: allows for employee input. Employees should have the option to vary activities according to personal needs, work habits, and the circumstances in the workplace. gives employees a sense of accomplishment. includes training so employees know what tasks to do and how to do them properly. provides good work/rest schedules. allows for an adjustment period for physically demanding jobs. provides feedback to the employees about their performance. minimizes energy expenditure and force requirements. balances static and dynamic work. Job design is an ongoing process. The goal is to make adjustments as conditions or tasks change within the workplace.

Ans. 24.

Achieving good job design involves administrative practices that determine what the employee does, for how long, where, and when as well as giving the employees choice where ever possible. In job design, you may choose to examine the various tasks of an individual job or the design of a group of jobs. Approaches to job design include: Job Enlargement: Job enlargement changes the jobs to include more and/or different tasks. Job enlargement should add interest to the work but may or may not give employees more responsibility. Job Rotation: Job rotation moves employees from one task to another. It distributes the group tasks among a number of employees. Job Enrichment: Job enrichment allows employees to assume more responsibility, accountability, and independence when learning new tasks or to allow for greater participation and new opportunities. Work Design (Job Engineering): Work design allows employees to see how the work methods, layout and handling procedures link together as well as the interaction between people and machines.

Ans. 25.
Goals can be in many difference areas and include: Task Variety To alleviate boredom, avoid both excessive static body positions and repetitive movements. Design jobs to have a variety of tasks that require changes in body position, muscles used, and mental activities.

Two methods are job enlargement and job rotation. For example, if an employee normally assembles parts, the job may be enlarged to include new tasks such as work planning, inspection/quality control, or maintenance. Alternatively, the tasks may include working in the same department, but changing tasks every hour. For example, in a laundry facility employees can rotate between various stations (sorting, washer, dryer, iron, etc) as long as it provides for a change in physical or mental expenditure.

Ans. 26.
Functional information systems include:
- Accounting Information Systems
- Marketing Information Systems
- Enterprise Information Systems
- Decision Support Information Systems
- Executive Information Systems
- Quality Management Information Systems
- Manufacturing Information Systems
- Financial Information Systems
- Human resource Information Systems

Ans. 27.
The Objective is to Provide the Management, A Range of Business Intelligence Business Performance Management Business rules Data Mining Predictive analytics Purchase order request Enterprise Architecture Information technology management Knowledge Base Online analytical processing etc.

Ans. 28.

For Management, MIS:
- Provide Information for Decision Makers to Make Solutions for the Most Challenging Situations.
- Provide Information for Making Strategic Decisions in a Competitive Situation.
- Provide Information for Strategic Planning
- Provide Information for Corporate Planning
- Provide Information for Business Planning
- Provide Information for Marketing Planning
- Provide Information for Industry Benchmarking
- Provide Information for Process Engineering
- Provide Information for Pricing Management
- Provide Information for Revenue Management
- Provide Information for Developing Strategic Alliances
- Provide Information for Allocating of Resources
- Provide Information for Resource Management
- Provide Information for Management Information Systems
- Provide Information for Identifying strategic shifts and positioning with clients in anticipation of several possible outcomes-scenario planning-is a core part of our strategic and tactical planning.
- Provide Information to see changes in market conditions, technical advances, and economic issues will all affect the industry/business in the future
- Provide Information to find the most effective marketing strategies in order to succeed in these challenging times
- Provide Information for Proprietary Databases and Analytical Support.
- Provide Information on Economic Conditions-past/Present/Future.
- Provide Information that enables to provide valuable understanding of the opportunities, challenges, potential pitfalls and market implications
- Provide Information which helps organizations realize the most value from their assets.

- Provides Information to Conduct portfolio management, remarketing assistance, sale and lease negotiations asset sourcing and acquisition, appraisal and valuation, auditS and management and expert testimony.
- Provide the Right Information for a clear and disciplined approach to financial planning is vital to ensure success.
- Provide Information for Objective Planning.
- Provide Information for the execution of effective business planning and sound management usually defines these differences in profitability.
- Provide Information to analyze and prioritize the BUSINESS drivers to help to achieve a superior competitive position. Vital to this process is an understanding of the economic advantages of scale and scope.
- Provides Information for Operational excellence results in the attainment of worldclass quality and productivity in the delivery of services to customers
- Provides Information to develop a clear understanding of their operating practices and associated costs particularly relative to competitors.

When running a business, the right information systems can have a critical impact operating costs, operating effectiveness, and customer satisfaction.

Ans. 29.

The major expectations of MIS are to: reach an understanding of the relevant processes on the basis of the available historic information. This element forms the basis for the development of models, required for forecasting and simulation. provide information on current situation, especially for early warning purposes, for instance related to issues impacting on business, resources or business status. forecast changes and impacts, either natural or man-made, as an element in vulnerability assessments. forecast the consequences of policy decisions and measures before they are implemented in reality. This implies evaluating options for several given scenarios based on the possible results and predicted consequences, and selecting the most acceptable alternative.

Ans. 30.
The Success/Failure of MIS Depends on Two Factors:
1. MIS developers
- ❖ done a through needs analysis for information requirements.
- ❖ tailor the information system for the organization requirements.
- ❖ user friendly

2. Users
- ❖ all managers/staff are well trained to use the information.
- ❖ the benefits are evaluated.

Ans. 31.
mean- (25000*5+60000*2+255000)/8= 62500 the employees earn less than the mean= 7 median= 8/2= 4th position mean's 25000.

Ans. 32.
One die will have a 1/6 chance of rolling a 1, 2.3, 4, 5 or 6.
The other die will have a 1/2 chance of rolling a 0 and 1/2 chance of rolling a 6.
This divides the total into two groups of total spots.
1: Die two has no spots, so the total is 1, 2, 3, 4, 5, or 6.
d in these challenging
2 Die two has six spots, so the total is 7, 8,9, 10, 11, or 12
Each of the numbers in each of the choices (1 or 2) is equally likely, and being in 1 or 2 is equally likely, so all of the
numbers from 1 to 12 is equally likely. This means that they each have a probability of 1/12
What this comes down to is Y is in {1,2,3,4,5,6,7,8,9,10,11,12}, all with equal chance so occurring. As we just stated, the
probability of each is 1/12.

Ans.33.

I would calculate the standard deviation on the entire set of numbers. I would then average the breast fed and the formula groups separately. Using the standard deviation, divide the difference in the average by that number. The would give you how many standard deviations there are between the two.

Using a one-sided normal table, you can look up the number of standard deviations you have as a probability of getting this difference.

1. The null hypothesis is that the mean globulin level is higher among breast-fed babies. The alternative hypothesis is that there is that there is no difference.
2. Find a one side normal table and look up the probability.
Also, 95% puts you at about 1.645 standard deviations.

Ans, 34.

Seasonal Indices are a compilation of daily seasonal values for individual commodities. A seasonal index rating is calculated for each of the average 251 trading days per year using the vast data resources that are provided with Unfair Advantage. Some of the resulting indices are virtually mirror images of the recent past, while others reflect only subtle seasonal effects. Seasonal indices offer a way to combine seasonal information on commodity data with daily chart analysis to promote a better understanding of price movement.

The seasonal index represents a + or -3 sigma confidence interval over time. It reflects and reports upon the entire
history of the series given as input in a cumulative manner. In the nonamplified form, the index is painted a day at a time as more input contributes to the seasonal pattern. The index may become more and more dampened as more information is supplied. There is no attempt to use the final year in the seasonal waveform to explain the past. In other words, the seasonal wave for of, say, a ten to 20 year series can be used as an input to forecast future events or simulate past events without bias where any then-current reading does not and cannot affect earlier seasonal patterns Improved results may appear when longer term computed input is prepared using the "detrend" option.

Seasonal Variation is a component of a time series which is defined as the repetitive and predictable movement around the trend line in one year or less. It is detected by measuring time intervals in small units, such as days, weeks months or quarters.

Organizations facing seasonal variations, like the motor vehicle industry is often interested in knowing their relative performance to the normal seasonal variation. Same is with the ministry of employment which expects unemployment to increase in June because recent graduates are just arriving into the market and also schools have also been given a vacation for the summer. The moot point is whether the increase is more or less than expected.

Organizations affected by seasonal variation need to identify and measure this seasonality to help with planning for

temporary increases or decreases in labor requirements, inventory, training, periodic maintenance, and so forth. Apart from these the organizations need to know if the seasonal variation they experience at more or less than the average rate.

Ans. 35.

The McKinsey 7S Framework

Ensuring that all parts of your organization work in harmony How do you go about analyzing how well your organization is positioned to achieve its intended objective? This is a question that has been asked for many years, and there are many different answers. Some approaches look at internal factors, others look at external ones, some combine these perspectives, and others look for congruence between various aspects of the organization being studied. Ultimately, the issue comes down to which factors to study.

The 7S model can be used in a wide variety of situations where an alignment perspective is useful, for example to help you:

- Improve the performance of a company;
- Examine the likely effects of future changes within a company;
- Align departments and processes during a merger or acquisition; or
- Determine how best to implement a proposed strategy.

The Seven Elements

The McKinsey 7S model involves seven interdependent factors which are categorized as either "hard" or "soft elements:
- Hard Elements -strategy/ Structure/Systems
- Soft Elements --shared Values/Style/Staff/Skills.

1. "Hard" elements are easier to define or identify and management can directly influence them: These are strategy statements; organization charts and reporting lines; and formal processes and IT systems.

2. "Soft" elements, on the other hand, can be more difficult to describe, and are less tangible and more influenced by culture. However, these soft elements are as important as the hard elements if the organization is going to be successful.

The way the model is presented in Figure 1 below depicts the interdependency of the elements and indicates how a change in one affects all the others. Let's look at each of the elements specifically:

1. Strategy: the plan devised to maintain and build competitive advantage over the competition.
2. Structure: the way the organization is structured and who reports to whom.
3. Systems: the daily activities and procedures that staff members engage in to get the job done.
4. Shared Values: called "superordinate goals" when the model was first developed, these are the core values of the company that are evidenced in the corporate culture and the general work ethic.
5. Style: the style of leadership adopted.
6. Staff: the employees and their general capabilities.
7. Skills: the actual skills and competencies of the employees working for the company.

How to Use the Model

Now you know what the model covers, how can use it?

The model is based on the theory that, for an organization to perform well, these seven elements need to be aligned
and mutually reinforcing. So, the model can be used to help identify what needs to be realigned to improve performance, or to maintain alignment (and performance) during other types of change.

Whatever the type of change- restructuring, new processes, organizational merger, new systems, change of leadership and so on - the model can be used to understand how the organizational elements are interrelated, and so ensure that the wider impact of changes made in one area is taken into consideration.

You can use the 7S model to help analyze the current situation (Point A), a proposed future situation (Point B) and to identify gaps and inconsistencies between them. It's then a question of adjusting and tuning the elements of the 7S model to ensure that your organization works effectively and well once you reach the desired endpoint.

Ans. 36.

Here are some of the questions that you'll need to explore to help you understand your situation in terms of the 7S framework.

1. Strategy
   - What is our strategy?
   - How to we intend to achieve our objectives?
   - How do we deal with competitive pressure?
   - How are changes in customer demands dealt with?
   - How is strategY adjusted for environmental issues?

2. Structure
   - How is the company/team divided?
   - What is the hierarchy?
   - How do the various departments coordinate activities?
   - How do the team members organize and align themselves?
   - Is decision making and controlling centralized or decentralized?
   - Is this as it should be, given what we're doing?
   - Where are the lines of communication?
   - Explicit and implicit?

3. Systems
   - What are the main systems that run the organization?
   - Consider financial and HR systems as well as communications and document storage. Where are the controls and how are they monitored and evaluated?
   - What internal rules and processes does the team use to keep on track?

4. Shared Values
   - What are the core values?
   - What is the corporate/team culture?
   - How strong are the values?
   - What are the fundamental values that the company/ team was built on?

5. Style
    - How participative is the management/leadership style?
    - How effective is that leadership? Do employees/team members tend to be competitive or cooperatrve?
    - Are there real teams functioning within the organization
    - or are they just nominal groups?
6. Staff
    - What positions or specializations are represented within the team?
    - What positions need to be filled? Are there gaps in required competencies?
7. Skills
    - What are the strongest skills represented within the company/team?
    - Are there any skills gaps?
    - What is the company/team known for doing well?
    - Do the current employees/team members have the ability to do the job?
    - How are skills monitored and assessed?

Ans. 37.
This is reference to the Indian political scene.
1. With the formation of the "Coalition" government at the centre, with the help of smaller regional partes, the focus was development of industries regionally. These regional parties, using their local pulls, developed industries with the help of industries. This was the reason for the fast growth of industries in regions like:
    - Tamil Nadu
    - Karnataka
    - Gujarat
    - Haryana, Etc. etc.
2. With the formation of the "Coalition" government at the centre, with the help of smaller regional parties, the focus was development of industries regionally. These regional parties, use the panchayat raj development programs to stimulate small businesses. Then with the intraduction of "microfinance", the small business, like one man business or employing few people thrived.

Today, There are Over 40 Million Small Businesses.

Ans. 38.

Retrenchment Strategy

Retrenchment is a corporate-level strategy that seeks to reduce the size or diversity of an organization's operations. Retrenchment is also a reduction of expenditures in order to become financially stable.

Retrenchment occurs when an organization regroups through cost and asset reduction to reverse declining sales and profits. This strategy is design to fortify an organization's basic distinctive competence. In some case, bankruptcy can be an effective type of retrenchment strategy. Bankruptcy can allow a firm to avoid major debt obligations and to avoid union contracts.

Corporate Retrenchment Strategies

Reduce scope of diversification to a smaller number of businesses
1. Certain businesses can't be made profitable
2. Diversification efforts have become too broad & building strong positions in fewer businesses is key to improving long-term performance Retrenchment revolves around cutting sales.

Retrenchment is a corporate-level strategy that seeks to reduce the size or diversity of an organization's operations. Retrenchment is also a reduction of expenditures in order to become financially stable. Retrenchment is a pullback or a withdrawal from offering some current products or serving some markets. In a military sibuation a retrenchment provides a second line of defense. Retrenchment is often a strategy employed prior to or as part of a Turnaround strategy.

There are five activities that characterize retrenchment:

Captive Company: Essentially, a captive company's destiny is tied to a larger company. For some companies, the only way to stay viable is to act as an exclusive supplier to a giant company. A company may also be taken captive if their competitive position is irreparably weak.

Turnaround: If your company is steadily losing profit or market share, a turnaround strategy may be needed. There are two forms of turnarounds: First, one may choose contractions (cutting labor costs, etc. Second, they may decide to consolidate.

Bankruptcy: This may also be a viable legal protective strategy. Bankruptcy without a customer base is truly a bad place. However, if one declares bankruptcy with loyal customers, there is at least a possibility of a turnaround.

Divestment: This is a form of retrenchment strategy used by businesses when they downsize the scope of their business activities. Divestment usually involves eliminating a portion of a business. Firms may elect to sell, close, or spin-off a strategic business unit, major opereting division, or product line. This move often is the final decision to eliminate unrelated, unprofitable, or unmanageable operations.

Liquidation: This is very simple. Take the book value of assets, subtract depreciation and sell the business. This may be hard for some companies to do because there may be untapped potential in the assets

Ans. 39.

Concentric Diversification

Type of diversification where a firm acquires or develops new products or services (closely related to its core business or technology) to enter one or more new markets.

Concentric diversification results when the new products are related to current products but are introduced into new
markets.

Concentric diversification: a growth strategy in which a company seeks to develop by adding new, but related, products to its existing product lines to attract new customers. See Conglomerate Diversification; Horizontal Diversification. Concentric diversification results in new product lines or services that have technological and/or marketing synergies with existing product lines, even though the products may appeal to a new customer group.

Conceutric Diversification: Conglomerate Diversification. Horizontal Integration a strategy for growth in which a company develops by seeking ownership of, or some measure of control over, some of its competitors.

Ans. 40.

The Boston Consulting Group Box ("BCG Box") Using the BCG Box, a company classifies all its business unit's according to two dimensions:

On the horizontal axis: relative market share-this serves as a measure of SBU strength in the market on the vertical axis: market growth rate - this provides a measure of market attractiveness By dividing the matrix into four areas, four types of SBU can be distinguised:

Stars:Stars are high growth businesses or products competing in markets where they are relatively strong compared with the competition. Often they need heavy investment to sustain their growth. Eventually their growth will slow and, assuming they maintain their relative market share, will become cash cows.

Cash Cows: Cash Cows are low-growth businesses or products with a relatively high market share. These are mature, successful businesses with relatively little need for investment. They need to be managed for continued profit – so that they continue to generate the strong cash flows that the company needs for its Stars.

Question marks: Question marks are businesses or products with low market share but which operate in higher growth markets. This suggests that they have potential, but may require substantial investment in order to grow market share at the expence of more powerful competitors. Management have to think hard about "question marks" – which ones should they invest in? Which ones should they allow to fail or shrink?

Dogs: Unsurprisingly, the term "dogs" refers to businesses or products that have low relative share in unattractive, low-growth markets. Dogs may generate enough cash to break-even, but they are rarely, if ever, worth investing in.

Ans. 41.
Contributions:
- Scientific approach to business management and process improvement
- Importance of compensation for performance
- Began the careful study of tasks and jobs
- Importance of selection criteria by management

Perspective of improving the productivity and efficiency of manual workers.

Ans. 42.
Profitability, productivily, morale and quality of work life are of concern to most organizations because they impact achievement of organization goals. There is an increasing trend to maximize an organization's investment in its employees. Jobs that previously required physical dexterity now require more mental effort. Organizations need to "work smarter" and apply creative ideas. The work force has also changed. Employees expect more from a day's work than simply a day's pay. They want challenge, recognition, a sense of accomplishment, worthwhile tasks and meaningful relationships with their managers and co-workers. When these needs are not met, performance declines. Today's customers demand continually improving quality, rapid product or service delivery; fast turn-around time on changes, competitive pricing and other features that are best achieved in complex environments by innovative organizational practices. The effective organization must be able to meet today's and tomorrow's challenges.

Adaptability and responsiveness are essential to survive and thrive. There are seven characteristics of OD: <u>Humanistic Values</u>: Positive beliefs about the potential of employees. <u>Systems Orientation</u>: All parts of the organization, to include structure, technology, and people, must work together. <u>Experiential Learning</u>: The learners' experiences in the training environment should be the kind of human problems they encounter at work. The training should NOT be all theory and lecture. <u>Problem Solving</u>: Problems are identified, data is gathered, corrective action is taken, progress is assessed, and adjustments in the problem solving process are made as needed. This process is known as Action Research. <u>Contingency Orientation:</u> Actions are selected and adapted to fit the need. <u>Change Agent</u>: Stimulate, facilitate, and coordinate change. <u>Levels ef Interventions</u>: Problems can occur at one or more level in the organization so the strategy will require one or more interventions.

Ans. 43.

To assist in recruitment needs, it is essential to have flexible service that allows an organization to recruit candidates all year long.

Job Postings:

Job pastings must be related to one or more academic programs. In addition, job postings must be of substance and not means to sell a service or product.

All interview questions must be job-related Disregard for these terms will result in termination of all recruitment relationships. During on-campus visits, no recruiter should schedule an interview without approval. Recruiters agree that resumes received for specific purposes cannot be provided to any other party without prior approval. as written in the Family Educational Rights and Privacy Act (FERPA).

Ans. 44.

The benefits HR outsourcing include:
- Skilled professionals to do the job
- Improved employee relations
- Money saved by cutting overall expenses

Benefits Administration: This can include things such as health benefits, vacation, sick leave, and retirement.

Risk Management: A vital area that has to do with insurance, primarily workers' compensation insurance.

Ans. 45.

Performance appraisal, also known as employee appraisal, is a method by which the job performance of an employee is evaluated (generally in terms of quality, quantity, cost and time). Performance appraisal is a part of career development. Performance appraisals are regular reviews of employee performance within organizations Generally, the aims of a performance appraisal are to:
1. Give feedback on performance to employees.
2. Identify employee training needs.
3. Document criteria used to allocate organizational rewards
4. Form a basis for personnel decisions: salary increases, promotions, disciplinary actions, etc.
5. Provide the opportunity for organizational diagnosis and development.
6. Facilitate communication between employee and administrator.
7. Validate selection techniques and human resource policies to meet federal Equal

Ans. 46.

Analysis of jobs in the organization is a primary task for setting a baseline that enables human resources (HR) professionals to effectively manage job-related activities. Job analysis consists of two components: job description and job speciftication (ôHRD & Marketingö). The job description óstates job related details such as duties and responsibilities, salary and incentives, working conditions and facilities, etc.,ö whereas the job specification ôgives the related details like qualifications and qualities required by job holders, experience and training required, etc. ö (ôHRD & Marketingö). A job analysis is an efficient way to gather useful information about a job, and its cost- effectiveness makes it affordable for any organization (Adams).

Any attempt to apply HR resources and talent to the organization Es jobs will be more effective if those jobs are

clearly specified in terms of their variables. An effective training program for a particular job cannot be developed unless information about what the job entails is elucidated, for example. Details about the job/Es content, systems, standards, and demands can be used to choose or develop a training program that specifically meets the needs of the

employees (Adams). A job analysis is useful for many reasons. It can facilitate employee performance evaluations and promotions by identifying the level of work the employee has been accomplishing well and specifying the level of work required for the new job.

Ans. 47.

A process which anticipates and maps out the consequences of business strategy on an organization's human resources. This is reflected in planning of skill and competence needs as well as total headcounts. For resourcing strategies to be implemented they must be translated into practical action. The strategic process can be organized logically-for example, following the decision sequence shown on page 351 of Human Resource Management in a Business Context. For these decisions to be taken, information must be obtained, consequences gauged, political soundings taken and preferences assessed.

It is clear that many of these decisions are fundamental to an organization. If the implications are major, strategic decisions are taken at the centre of the business. The role of the human resource function is twofold:

1. To participate in the decision process by providing information and opinion on each option, including:
   - redundancy or recruitment costs
   - consequences on morale
   - redeployment/outplacement opportunities
   - availability of skilled staff within the organization
   - availability of suitable people in the job market
   - time constraints
   - development/training needs/schedules
   - management requirements.

This forms part of the information collated from the organization as a whole The first step for IT human resources
planning is to determine which jobs are classified as 'information technology occupations' .3 This, however, is not a
simple task. As Freeman and Aspray(1999) noted: "[IT occupations] vary enormously in the technical and other skills required for the job. These jobs are not located solely in the IT industry (the industry whose primary business is to make and sell IT devices, software, services and systems), and they do not always involve the design and creation of information technology artefacts. Instead, they are distributed throughout virtually every sector of society, including government, all sectors of industry and most non-profit organizations; and they may involve many people who propose, implement, enhance and maintain systems that rely upon information technology. Not every job in an IT company is necessarily IT work (Are the janitors at IBM IT workers? We think not). Many jobs involve some contact with information technology, not all would be considered IT jobs; otherwise, this category would soon become so large as to be useless."

Ans. 48.

Knowledge is defined variously as
1. facts, information, and skills acquired by a person through Experience or Education; the theoretical or practical understanding of a subject,
2. what is known in a particular field or in total; facts and information or
3. awareness or familiarity gained by experience of a fact or situation.

Knowledge acquisition involves complex Cognitive processes: perception, learning, communication, association and reasoning. The term knowledge is also used to mean the confident understanding of a subject with the ability to use it for a specific purpose. We define knowledge management as a business activity with two primary aspects: Treating the knowledge component of business activities as an explicit concern of business reflected in strategy, policy, and practice at all levels of the organization. Making a direct connection between an organization'S intellectual assets - both explicit (recorded] and tacit [personal know-how] - and positive business results.

Ans.49.

Marketplaces are increasingly competitive and the rate of innovation is rising. Reductions in staffing create a need to replace informal knowledge with formal methods. Competitive pressures reduce the size of the work force that holds valuable business knowledge. The amount of time available to experience and acquire knowledge has diminished. Early retirements and increasing mobility ol the work force lead to loss of knowledge. There is a need to manage increasing complexity as small operating companies are transnational sourcing operations. Changes in strategic direction may result in the loss of knowledge in a specific area. Most of our work is information based. Organizations compete on the basis of knowledge.

Products and services are increasingly complex, endowing them with a significant information component. The need for life -long learning is an inescapable reality. In brief, knowledge and information have become the medium in which business problems occur. As a result, managing knowledge represents the primory opportunity for achieving substantial savings significant improvements in human performance, and competitive advantage. It's not just a Fortune 500 business problem. Small companies need formal approaches to knowledge management even more, because they don't have the market leverage, inertia, and resources that big companies do. They have to be much more flexible, more responsive, and more "right" (make better decisions) - because even small mistakes can be fatal to them.

Ans. 50.
Vertical: Boundaries between layers within an organization Classic Example: Military organization Problem: Someone in a lower layer has a useful idea; "Chain of command" mentality.

Horizontal: Boundaries which exist between organizations functional units. Each unit has a singular function. Problem: Each unit maximize their own goals but not the overall goal of the organization

External: Barriers between the organization and the outside world (customers, suppliers, other government entities, special interest groups, communities). Customers are the most capable of identifying major problems in the organizations and are interested in solutions. Problem: Lose sight of the customer needs and supplier requirements

Geographic: Barriers among organizations units located in different Problem: Isolation of innovative practices and ideas

Ans. 51.
One that makes all of these barriers much more permeable than they are now; loosen boundaries Let information/ ideas/resources/energy flow throughout the organization and into others.

Ans. 52.
No-there will always have some hierarchy, functional divisions, geographic boundaries, limits between organizations.

Ans. 53.
- It removes many barriers - especially that of time and location.
- It emphasizes concentrating on new services and products, especially those with intensive information and knowledge
- characteristics, rather than concentrating on cost savings made possible by removing the barriers.
- It goes beyond outsourcing and strategic alliances and is more flexible in: that it has continuously changing partners, the arrangements are loose and goal oriented, emphasizes the use of knowledge to create new products and services, Its processes can change quickly by agreement of the partners.

Ans. 54.
The company has the following functional departments
- marketing
- manufacturing
- sales
- finance/administration
- human resource
- customer service
- distribution
- warehousing/transportation
- TQM

Ans. 55.
Division of labor: dividing up the many tasks of the organization into specialized jobs.
Hierarchy of authority: Who manages whom.
Span of control: Who manages whom?
Line vs staff positions
Decentralization
Hierarchy of Authority
Tall vs flat hierarchies
Autonomy and control
Communication
Size
Span of Control
A wide span of control: a large number of employees reporting, A narrow span of control: a small number employees reporting. The appropriate span of control depends on the experience, knowledge and skills of the employees and the nature of the task.
Line vs Staff Positions
Line positions are those in which people are involved in producing the main goods or service or make decisions relating to the production of the main business. Staff positions These are positions in which people make recommendations to others but are not directly involved in the production of the good or service.
Decentralization
The extent to which decision making is concentrated in a few people or dispersed through out the organization
Advantage: benefits associated with greater participation and moving the decision closest towards implementation Disadvantage: Lack of perspective and information, lack of consensus.

Ans. 56.

The human relations approach recognised the need to design jobs in an interesting manner. In the past two decades much work has been directed to changing jobs so that job incumbents can satisfy their needs for growth, recognition and responsibilility, enhancing need satisfaction through what is called job enrichment. One widely publicised approach to job enrichment uses what is called job characteristics model and this has been explained separately in the ensuing section.

Two types of factors, viz.
1. motivators like achievements, recognition, work itself, responsibility, advancement and growth
2. hygiene factors (which merely maintain the employee on the job and in the organization) like working conditions, organizational policies, inter-personnel relations, pay and job security.

The employee is dissatisfied with the job if maintenance factors to the required degree are not introduced into the job. But, the employee may not be satisfied even if the required maintenance factors are provided. The employee will be satisfied with his job and he will be more productive if motivators are introduced into the job content. As such, he asserts that the job designer has to introduce hygienic factors adequately to reduce dissatisfaction and build motivating factors. Thus, THE emphasis is on the psychological needs of the employees in designing jobs.

Ans. 57.

The Job Characteristics Theory states that employees will work hard when they are rewarded for the work they do and when the work gives them satisfaction. Hence, they suggest that motivation, satisfaction and performance should be integrated in the job design. According to this approach, any job can be described in terms of five core job dimensions which are defined as follows:

1. Skill variety: The degree to which the job requires that workers use a variety of different activities, talents and kills in order to successfully complete the job requirements.
2. Task identity: The degree to which the job allows workers to complete whole tasks from start to finish, rather than disjointed portions of the job.
3. Task significance: The degree to which the job significantly impacts the lives of others both within and outside the workplace.

4. Autonomy The degree to which the job allows workers freedom in planning and scheduling and the methods used to complete the job.
5. Feedback: The degree to which the job itself provides workers with clear, direct and understandable knowledge of their performance.

All of the job dimensions impact workers psychologically. The first three dimensions affect whether or not workers view their job as meaningful. Autonomy determines the extent of responsibility workers feel. Feedback allows for feelings of satisfaction for a job well done by providing knowledge of results.

Ans. 58.
Rest breaks help alleviate the problems of unavoidable repetitive movements or static body positions. More frequent but shorter breaks (sometimes called 'micro breaks") are sometimes preferable to fewer long breaks. During rest breaks, encourage employees to change body position and to exercise. It is important that employees stretch and use different muscle groups. If the employee has been very active, a rest break should include a stationary activity or stretching, Allowance for an Adjustment Period

Ans. 59.
MIS is an integrated information system, which is used to provide management with needed information on a regular basis.
The term system in MIS implies Order, Arrangement, and Purpose.
The information can be used for various purposes,
- Strategic planning
- Delivering increased productivity
- reducing service cycles
- reducing product development cycles
- reducing marketing life cycles
- increasing the understanding of customers needs
- facilitating business and process re-engineering.

MIS can also be used across the organization as an information utility to
- support policy making
- meet regulatory and legislative requirements
- support research and development
- support consistent and rapid decision making
- enable effective and efficient utilization of resources
- provide evidence of business transactions
- identify and manage risks
- evaluate and document quality, performance and achievements.

Ans. 60.
Technology refers to the application of knowledge and tools to solve problems and achieve more efficiency. It represents powerful forces that influence human lives in important ways. Whenever a new technology shows its impact, many existing technologies become obsolete. However, a new technology may not always prove to be advantageous, unless the new technology creates successful products.

Chapter Three - Long Questions

Q 1 Discuss the concept of competency mapping. Briefly explain the methods of competency mapping taking suitable examples.

Q 2 Summarize the recent trend of reward systems in India. Discuss its impact on productivity.

Q 3 Define and discuss the need of human resource planning.

Q 4 What are the forms and causes of indiscipline in an organization?

Q 5 Define HRM and differentiate it from traditional personnel management.

Q 6 "For Management Movement to develop it is essential that there should be emphasis on participative management." Analyze this statement.

Q 7 "The sectoral contributions of the three sectors namely primary, secondary and teritary to the national income and employment have changed over a period." Briefly explain the above statement in the context of structural changes in the economy.

Q 8 How would you apply your knowledge of marketing concept to create awareness and communicate the perils in Sale driving habit and smoking.

Q 9 Packaging is considered as the fifth "P" of the Marketing Mix. What makes it so? Bring out the strategic importance and relevance as a vital tool of product decisions.

Q 10 Visit some of the organizations to identify the information systems used for the better management. Suggest the ways and means for the improvement.

Q 11 Discuss various types of organizational changes

Q 12 What is a chi-square test? How do you find the degrees of freedom in a chi-square distribution? Discuss chi-square test as a test for goodness of fit and as a test of independence.

Q 13 Managerial Economics serves as a "link between traditional economics and decision making sciences." Discuss.

Q 14 "The main determinant of elasticity is the availability of subtitutes." Explain this statement in the contest of price elasticity of demand.

Q 15 "Oligopoly is the most prevalent form of market structure in the manufacturing sector." Describe this statement.

Q 16 Discuss the universal perspectives of Organisational Design.

Q 17 Explain the contemporary approaches to job design.

Q 18 Define organizational diagnosis. Discuss different methods of organizational analysis.

Q 19 Write an essay on the process of change and enumerate how it is carried out in an organization you are familiar with. Briefly describe the organisation you are referring to.

Q 20 After ten years of struggle, a company manufacturing radio sets and computers, surfaced in 1982-83 to make a profit of Rs 64 lakhs and then Rs. 1.14 crores in 1983-84, but again slipped back to Rs. 1.10 crore losses in the accounting period that followed. It is reported that the company's radio division was unlikely ever to pay its way, its computers failed to make a splash, and its earlier efforts to diversify were yet to bear fruit. According to high level executive, the company concentrated on manufacturing when it needed a marketing orientation. When a new CEO was appointed, his remedy for revival was to divisonalise the organization, introduce more accountability and diversify into direct to home television (DTH) and other areas.
(i) Analyze as to what went wrong with the implementation of the company's strategy?
(ii) Critically comment on the measures of revival suggested by the new CEO.

Q 21 Explain the concept of a career. Describe the strategies adopted for career development in your organization or any organization you are familiar with. Briefly describe the organization you are referring to.

Q 22 What are different work practices which promote learning?

Q 23 Explain the reasons for the growth of private sector.

Q 24 What are the main components of network?

Q 25 Explain why portfolio analysis is necessary in the case of multi-product organizations

Q 26 What is human resource cost? Discuss the measurement of human resource cost in your organization or any organization you are familiar with. Describe the organization you are referring to.

Q 27 Discuss the objectives of performance appraisal. Describe the method of performance appraisal being used in an organization you are acquainted with. Describe the organization you are referring to.

Q 28 Do you believe that KM can improve the competitiveness of a firm?

Q 29 Write a detailed note on the advantages of networks.

Q 30 What are the different approaches to organisation?

Chapter Three - Answers to Long Questions

Ans.1.
Competency mapping is a process through which one assesses and determines one's strengths as an individual worker and in some cases, as part of an organization. It generally examines two areas: emotional intelligence or emotional quotient (EQ), and strengths of the individual in areas like team structure, leadership, and decision-making. Large organizations frequently employ some form of competency mapping to understand how to most effectively employ the competencies of strengths of workers. They may also use competency mapping to analyze the combination of strengths in different workers to produce the most effective teams and the highest quality work.

Competency mapping can also be done for contract or freelance workers, or for those seeking employment to emphasize the specific skills which would make them valuable to a potential employer. These kinds of skills can be determined, when one is ready to do the work, by using numerous books on the subject. One of the most popular ones is Now, Discover Your Strengths by Marcus Buckingham and Donald Clifton, initially published in 2001.

Buckingham and Clifton's book, and others like it, practice competency mapping through testing, having the person sift through past work experiences, and by analyzing learning types. However, the disadvantage to using a book alone is that most people may have a few blind spots when they analyze their own competency. Their perception of how others react to them may not be accurate.

Competency mapping also requires some thought, time, and analysis, and some people simply may not want to do the work involved to sufficiently map competencies. Thus a book like the above is often used with a human resources
team, or with a job coach or talented headhunter. Competency mapping alone may not produce accurate results unless one is able to detach from the results in analyzing past successes and failures. Many studies find that people often overestimate their abilities, making self competency mapping results dubious.

The value of competency mapping and identifying emotional strengths is that many employers now purposefully screen employees to hire people with specific competencies.

They may need to hire someone who can be an effective time leader or who has demonstrated great active listening skills. Alternately, they may need someone who enjoys taking initiative or someone who is very good at taking direction. When individuals must seek new jobs, knowing one's competencies can give one a competitive edge in the job market.

Usually, a person will find themselves with strengths in about five to six areas. Sometimes an area where strengths are not present is worth developing. In other cases, competency mapping can indicate finding work that is suited to one's strengths, or finding a department at one's current work where one's strengths or needs as a worker can be exercised. A problem with competency mapping, especially when conducted by an organization is that there may be no room for an individual to work in a field that would best make use of his or her competencies. If the company does not respond to competency mapping by reorganizing its employees, then it can be of little short-term benefit and may actually result in greater unhappiness on the part of individual employees.

A person identified as needing to learn new things in order to remain happy might find himself or herself in a position where no new training is ever required. If the employer cannot provide a position for an employee that fits him or her better, competency mapping may be of little use.

However, competency mapping can ultimately serve the individual who decides to seek employment in an environment where he or she perhaps can learn new things and be more intellectually challenged. Being able to list competencies on resumes and address this area with potential employers may help secure more satisfying work. This

may not resolve issues for the company that initially employed competency mapping, without making suggested changes. It may find competency mapping has produced dissatisfied workers or led to a high worker turnover rate.

Ans. 2.

The current trend is one of integrated reward approach. Reward system usually mean the financial reward on organization gives its employees in return for their labour. While the term reward system, not only includes material rewards, but also nonmaterial rewards. The components of a reward system consist of financial rewards (basic and performance pay) and employee benefits, which together comprise total remuneration. They also include non-financial rewards (recognition, promotion, praise, achievement responsibility and personal growth) and in many case a system of performance management. Pay arrangements are central to the cultural initiative as they are the most tangible expression of the working relationship between employer and employee.

The integrated reward system includes:

Job evaluation and profiling Defining key performance indicators Analysis and modification of pay levels and structures to reflect both internal and market relativities Designing of performance evaluation processes Structuring of individual, team and corporate performance bonuses Social climate surveys with focus on remuneration. Designing flexible benefits plans Implementation of new reward components in compensation package Implementation and assistance in change communications Training for internal specialists in reward structure planning and maintenance.

Performance Based Reward is based on the definition of key performance indicators identified as part of job evaluation, and linking these indicators with reward components. A combination of performance measuring system and additional motivational components delivers an integrated performance-based reward system.

Flexible Benefits Schemes are a modern approach to the management of budgets for staff remuneration. Employee benefits constitute a considerable portion of staff costs, but they are often expended without the desired effect since employees do not perceive the full values of benefits. This system increases the effectiveness and enable better control.

These components will be designed , developed and maintained on the basis of reward strategies and policies which will be created within the context of the organizations between strategies, culture and environment: they will be expected to fulfil the following broad aims;

1. Improve Organizational Effectiveness: Support the attainment of the organization's mission, strategies, and help to achieve sustainable, competitive advantage.
2. Support and change culture: Under pin and as necessary help to change the 'organizational culture' as expressed through its values for performance innovation, risks taking, quality, flexibility and team working.
3. Achieve Integration: Be an integrated part of the management process of the organization. This involves playing a key role in a mutually reinforcing and coherent range of personal policies and process.
4. Supportive Managers: Support individual managers in the achievement of their goals.
5. Motivate Employees : Motivate employees to achieve high levels of quality performance.
6. Compete in the Labour Market: Attract and retain high quality people.
7. Improved Skills : Upgrade competence and encourage personal development.
8. Improved Quality: Help to achieve continuous improvement in levels of quality and customer service.
9. Develop team working : Improve co-operation and effective team working at all level.
10. Value for money: Pride value for the money for the organization

The Reward systems focus on positive reinforcement. Positive reinforcement is the most effective tool for encouraging desired behavior because it stimulates people to take actions because they want to because they get something of value (internally or externally) for doing it. An effectively designed and managed reward program can drive an organization's change process by positively reinforcing desired behaviors.

The SMART criteria.

These criteria used when designing and evaluating programs. Programs should be: Specific. A line of sight should be maintained between rewards and actions. Meaningful. The achievements rewarded should provide an important return on investment to both the performer and the organization. Achievable. The employee's or group's goals should be within the reach of the performers. Reliable. The program should operate according to its principles and purpose.

Timely. The recognition/rewards should be provided frequently enough to make performers feel valued for their efforts.

Performance Management:

The process of performance management reflects how the work gets done and creates the environment in which people feel valued for their achievements. The performance management process includes four critical components:

Focus on what is important to change or be improved. Measures to determine whether and how much progress is being achieved. Feedback so that performers will know whether and how much progress is being achieved. Reinforcement so that everyone celebrates achievements as they are unfolding. Indicators of successful performance

management include the following: All measures are understood by the employees, who can describe the importance of their activities to the agency. Measures address results and behaviors/processes.

A tracking system is used to monitor performance in the areas identified. The performance measures and progress are displayed in a public area. Data on the performance charts is current. The team leaders/managers are actively engaged in coaching staff members and providing assistance to improve performance. Periodic celebrations mark achievements as they are realized These celebrations are regarded positively by employees. Data indicate performance is improving.

Recommend that organizations: focus on variables critical to success; create timely, chart-oriented feedback; create celebrations that mean something to the performers; use performance reviews as an opportunity to reflect "how we won" and "how we lost" make them as often as necessary to cement the learning; anchor the memory of achievements achievement-oriented firms measure a lot, accomplish milestones frequently, and do much celebrating; don't rely on annual performance appraisals as the sole source of feedback; when designing programs, avoid copying programs used by other organizations; and don't make the design process into the "let's make a form" game.

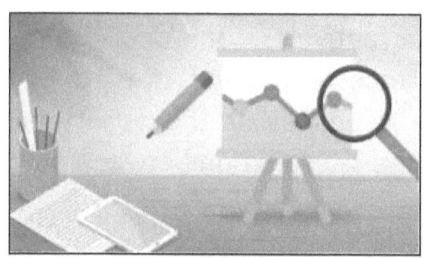

Ans .3.
When it concerns human resources, there are the more specific criticisms that it is over-quantitative and neglects the qualitative aspects of contribution. The issue has become not how many people should be employed, but ensuring that all members of staff are making an effective contribution. And for the future, the questions are what are the skills that will be required, and how will they be acquired.

There are others, though, that still regard the quantitative planning of resources as important. They do not see its value in trying to predict events, be they wars or takeovers. Rather, they believe there is a benefit from using planning to challenge assumptions about the future, to stimulate thinking. For some there is, moreover, an implicit or explicit wish to get better integration of decision making and resourcing across the whole organization, or greater influence by the centre over developed operating units.

Why human resource planning?

Human Resource Planning; an Introduction was written to draw these issues to the attention of HR or line managers. We address such questions as:

what is human resource planning?
- how do organizations undertake this sort of exercise?
- what specific uses does it have?

In dealing with the last point we need to be able to say to hard pressed managers: why spend time on this activity rather than the other issues bulging your in tray? The report tries to meet this need by illustrating how human resource planning techniques can be applied to four key problems. It then concludes by considering the circumstances is which human resourcing can be used.

1. Determining the numbers to be employed at a new location

If organisations overdo the size of their workforce it will carry surplus or underutilised staff. Alternatively, if the opposite misjudgement is made, staff may be overstretched, making it hard or impossible to meet production or service deadlines at the quality level expected. So the questions we ask are: the interrelation between productivity, work:

- ❖ How can output be improved your through understanding the interrelation between productivity, work organisation and technological development? What does this mean for staff numbers?
- ❖ What techniques can be used to establish workforce requirements?
- ❖ Have more flexible work arrangements been considered?
- ❖ How are the staff you need to be acquired? The principles can be workforce requirements, whether it be a business start-up, a relocation, or the opening of new factory or office.

2. Retaining your highly skilled staff

Issues about retention may not have been to the fore in recent years, but all it needs is for organisations to lose key staff to realise that an understanding of the pattern of resignation is needed. Thus organisations should:

- ❖ monitor the extent of resignation
- ❖ discover the reasons for it
- ❖ establish what it is costing the organisation
- ❖ compare loss rates with other similar organisations.

Without this understanding, management may be unaware of how many good quality staff are being lost. This will cost the organisation directly through the bill for separation, recruitment and induction, but also through a loss of long-term capability.

Having understood the nature and extent of resignation steps can be taken to rectify the situation. These may be relatively cheap and simple salutions once the reasons for the departure of employees have been identified. But it will depend on whether the problem is peculiar to your own organisation, and whether it is concentrated in particular groups (eg by age, gender, grade or skill).

3. Managing an effective downsizing programme

This is an all too common issue for managers. How is the workforce to be cut painlessly, while at the same time protecting the long-term interests of the organisation? A question made all the harder by the time pressures management is under, both because of business necessities and employee anxieties. HRP helps by considering:

- ❖ the sort of workforce envisaged at the end of the exercise
- ❖ the pros and cons of the different routes to get there
- ❖ how the nature and extent of wastage will change during the run-down
- ❖ the utility of retraining, redeployment and transfers
- ❖ what the appropriate recruitment levels might be.

Such an analysis can be presented to senior managers so that the cost benefit of various methods of reduction can be assessed, and the time taken to meet targets established.

If instead the CEO announces on day one that there will be no compulsory redundancies and voluntary severance is open to all staff, the danger is that an unbalenced workforce will result, reflecting, the take up of the severance offer. It is often difficult and expensive to replace lost quality and experience.

4. Where will the next generation of managers come from?

Many senior managers are troubled by this issue. They have seen traditional career paths disappear. They have had to bring in senior staff from elsewhere. But they recognise that while this may have dealt with a short-term skills shortage, it has not solved the longer term question of managerial supply: what sort, how many, and where will they come from? To address these questions you need to understand:

- ❖ the present career system (including patterns of promotion and movement, of recruitment and wastage)
- ❖ the characteristics of those who currently occupy senior positions
- ❖ the organisation's future supply of talent.
- ❖ recruiting to meet a shortage of those with senior management potential
- ❖ allowing faster promotion to fill immediate gaps
- ❖ developing cross functional transfers for high fliers
- ❖ hiring on fixed-term contracts to meet short-term skills/experience deficits
- ❖ reducing staff numbers to remove blockages or forthcoming surpluses.

Ans. 4.

Forms of Indiscipline:
- Talking out of turn (eg, by making remarks, calling out, distracting others by chattering)
- Calculated idleness and work avoidance (eg, delaying start to work set, not having essential equipment)
- Hindering other Employees (eg, by distracting them from work, interfering with equipment or materials)
- Not being punctual to work.
- Making unnecessary non-verbal noise (eg, by scraping chairs, banging objects, moving clumsily)
- Persistently infringing rules
- Cheeky or impertinent remarks or responses
- General rowdiness, horseplay or 'mucking about'
- Verbal abuse towards other employees (eg, offensive or insulting remarks)
- Physical aggression towards other emplayees (eg, by pushing, punching, striking)
- Verbal abuse towards the Managers/Supervisors (eg. offensive, insulting, insolent or threatening remarks)
- Physical destructiveness (eg, breaking objects, damaging furniture and fabric) etc.

Causes of Indiscipline:
- destructive behavior
- excessive naughtiness.
- habitually unorganized
- lack of concentration
- lack of confidence
- lack of attention
- low performance
- moody behavior
- non-participant behavior
- peer pressure
- stress
- weak memory.

Ans. 5.
Some experts assert that there is no difference between human resources and personnel management. They state that the two terms can be used interchangeably, with no difference in meaning. In fact, the terms are often used interchangeably in help-wanted ads and job descriptions.

For those who recognize a difference between personnel management and human resources, the difference can be described as philosophical. Personnel management is more administrative in nature, dealing with payroll, complying with employment law, and handling related tasks. Human resources, on the other hand, is responsible for managing a workforce as one of the primary resources that contributes to the success of an organization.

When a difference between personnel management and human resources is recognized, human resources is described as much broader in scope than personnel management. Human resources is said to incorporate and develop personnel management tasks, while seeking to create and develop teams of workers for the benefit of the organization. A primary goal of human resources is to enable employees to work to a maximum level of efficiency management.

Personnel management can include administrative tasks that are both traditional and routine. It can be described as reactive, providing a response to demands and concerns as they are presented By contrast, human resources involves ongoing strategies to manage and develop an organization's workforce.

It is proactive, as it involves the continuous development of functions and policies for the purposes of improving a company's workforce. Personnel management is often considered an independent function of an organization. Human resource management, on the other hand, tends to be an integral part of overall company function responsibility of an organization's personnel department.

Personnel management is typically the sole responsibility of an organization's personnel department. With human resources, all of an organization's managers are often involved in some manner, and a chief goal may be to have managers of various departments develop the skills necessary to handle personnel-related tasks.

As far as motivators are concerned, personnel management typically seeks to motivate employees with such things as compensation, bonuses, rewards, and the simplification of work responsibilities. From the personnel management point of view, employee satisfaction provides the motivation necessary to improve job performance. The opposite is true of human resources. Human management holds that improved performance leads to employee satisfaction. With human resources, work groups, effective strategies for meeting challenges, and job creativity are seen as the primary motivators.

Ans. 6.
Participative management is a method, which gives employees responsibility, accountability, and authority over their work. The method provides simple tools for employees to improve their work performance and positively impact the bottom line. The process provides an environment to make employee needs known and creates a vehicle for improved communication between all areas of the organization.

Participative management has clear goals and does not turn over the organization to employees. There is still a hierarchy but it is not a dominant hierarchy, which dictates everything to employees. A non-dominant hierarchy has as many levels as are necessary to do the work of the organization. People have clear roles and responsibilities and manage themselves as much as possible. Management tells people what the strategy is and what is expected in terms of results and then allows people to figure out the how to deliver on management expectations. Top management still decides strategy and front line employees still focus on their primary tasks. The difference is that the criteria for superior performance are utilized and leveraged for the success of the organization. The criteria for superior performance are drivers of behavior, reasons why people get up in the morning and are enthusiastic about their work. Pay is considered a satisfier all things being equal. The criteria for superior performance are:
- Control
- Learning
- Variety
- Mutual Support and Respect
- A Promising Future
- Engage one or several of their preferred life interests
- Challenges that match and stretch individual skills
- Concentration and Focus/ Fun

Participative management means Sharing Authority through delegation.
The Sharing (Delegating) Process:
Responsibility + Authority+ Accountability
Negotiate the Following Steps
- Goals: We start with the end in mind.
- Guidelines: We negotiate parameters, history, policies, boundaries, etc.
- Resources: We negotiate the money, equipment, supplies, human resources, time, and authority available.
- Accountability: We negotiate what information will be tracked, how, when, and to whom it will be reported.
- Reward: Unless there are special spifs, bonuses, or incentives, rewards usually include good reviews, higher raises, greater opportunity for promotion, greater autharity, etc.

Skills Required for Participative Management
1. Interest and concern. Some people prefer to be told what to do.
2. Recognize and enhance talents in others. Some people fear they will lose power if they build others.
3. Recognize and work around weaknesses in others. Some people are so irritated by deficiencies of others that they can't they can't recognize and work with their strengths.
4. Communication-particularly listening. We often would rather inform than become informed.
5. Conflict resolution. It is easier to create a conflict than to resolve one. It usually requires forgiving others-something most people don't do well.
6. Self-control. Getting the best out of others requires controlling our selves-our habits, anger, self-serving tendencies.
7. Negotiation. It can seem difficult to negotiate when we already have the power to simply decide and act.
8. Compromise. We often must compromise short-term personal or departmental goal to achieve a company goal or help another achieve a personal goal.
9. Synergy. The PM process relies on the belief that 1+1= 3.
10. Teachability. When the team answer is different than our preconceived desire we must learn from the team.
11. Flexibility. We must learn from others and then implement the better alternatives

12. Correction. The PM process constantly makes it clear that, "I was mistaken," "I didn't think of everything," "I wasn't considering another's viewpoint," etc. Most people don't like this process.

Benefits of Participative Management.
 1. Increase Productivity (Effectiveness and efficiency)
 2. Better Decisions
 3. Employee Morale
 1. Improved job satisfaction
 2. Greater Commitment
 3. Faster Adaptation to Change
 4. Greater trust
 5. Better Communication
 6. Better Teamwork

Participative Management Development
Phase 1: Initial Stages
- lack of challenges.
- lack of job satisfaction.
- non driven work environment.
- lack of team unity.
- low morale
- stagnant productivity.

Phase 2: Transition Stages
- clearly defined goals.
- proper feedback
- supporting work environment
- team building
- use of communication skills
- creative strategies
- improved production

Phase 3: Current Stages
- emphasis on performance
- thriving work environment
- team cohesiveness
- high morale
- innovative production

What Participative Management is not.
1. It is not permissiveness. PM holds people responsible.
2. It is not weakness. PM takes character to apply.
3. It is not involvement in trivia. Only significant decisions should go through the PM process, however, what one person sees as trivia may be very important to an other.
4. It does not mean giving up authority. We don't give up authority, rather we delegate authority with matching amounts of responsibility and accountability.
5. It does not mean giving up all decision making. We delegate only the amount of decision-making that we think is appropriate under the circumstances. Delegated authority may require a person to recommend action rather than take action.
6. It does not mean postponing action. PM should occur quickly and avoid constant fixes.

Management in most organizations is constantly attempting to get people more involved in improving the organization. People run up against a brick wall because of the bureaucratic structures that still exist in their organizations. This occurs even after many attempts at improvement.

Participative management enables organizations to improve performance through a fast, an economical method called the participative design workshop. It clearly states that the desigrn principle underlying the work is a participative method that has clear goals and simple tools for work process improvement. It can be utilized to improve the structure of the organization or just for work process improvement. This will depend on the needs of the organization.

Ans.7.

The sectoral contributions of the three sectors namely primary, secondary and tertiary to the national income and employment have changed over a period.

Economic Development and Sectoral Analysis:

The economy of any modern nation comprises of three basic sectors, namely-primary sector, secondary sector and tertiary sector. The primary sector comprises of agricultural and allied activities. Economic activities such as fishing, forestry, horticulture, bee-keeping etc. can be put together under the heading of allied actvities. Secondary sector mainly includes mining, industry and manufacturing.

The services sector comprises of community, social and personal services, insurance, finance, banking, shipping and transport. All these sectors are inter-related; any imbalance or shock in one sector can produce repercussions in the other two sectors.

Development of an economy can be judged in terms of the sectoral contribution of each of these sectors to the nation's total output and employment generated. In an underdeveloped economy, majority of the employment is generated by the primary sector. Also. Primary sector holds a large share in the total output (or Gross National Product) produced.

Since most of the people are engaged in agriculture, so we find that land (area-wise) to man (population-wise) ratio is quite low in agriculture for the underdeveloped countries compared to the developed countries. In such a situation, if agricultural land is concentrated (owned by) in few hands, then this will cause landlessness to majority of the people. There will be widespread poverty with very low purchasing power in the hands of majority of the rural population. State intervention in such a situation becomes important-first of all, to carry out land reforms (redistribution of land to the poor landless and marginal labourers and peasants, either by purchasing land from the land rich section and selling it at subsidized rates to the land poor section, or by 'radical land reforms' as was carried out in some countries such as China, where state took away the land from the land rich section without paying any economic compensation). One must know that fragmentation of land is a big problem in South Asian nations. Hence, sometimes it is said that land reforms can lead to lower output unless there is creation of land co-operatives or 'communes'. But this is difficult task. Formation of communes can fail if there is no trust among the land-owners. Countries where a majority of the population is engaged in agriculture are generally poor. But there are some exceptions such as Australia, New Zealand etc. Second of all, if land reforms were improperly implemented or could not be carried out, then the State can play a crucial role in the creation of the secondary sector (diversification), by investing in the secondary sector through deficit financing. This was done in the case of India during the 2nd and 3rd Five Year Plans based on the Mahalanobis model for industrialisation. However, the plans were criticised for neglecting the agricultural sector which led to food insecurity and later led to the adoption of green revolution.

It becomes necessary to expand the secondary sector for the following reasons:

1. Technological growth can take place in an economy which has a vibrant secondary sector. It is in the secondary sector where modern inputs such as fertilisers (chemical/ bio) are manufactured, which are crucial inputs for modern agriculture.

2. The newly developed industrial sector will become a new arena for generating employment, which can reduce the pressure on agricultural land. This can help in modernizing agriculture thru mechanisation (like using tractors, electrical harvesters). Again introduction of machines and new technology will raise the productivity of labour in agriculture and hence the purchasing power.

3. The growth of the secondary sector is bound to be greater than that of the primary sector in the initial phase because of its comparative advantage in terms of technology. This will lift up the gross output and place the economy in a new steady state growth path. But if the agricultural sector fails to catch up with the growing demand for food grains coming from the growing industrial sector, then this will lead to inflationary tendencies in the economy.

After an economy is already into the modern phase, it is essential to give a thrust to the tertiary sector. There is substantial amount of difference between the tertiary sector and the other two remaining sectors. In the tertiary sector, no tangible goods are produced. Tertiary sector do not produce anything but services. It is not involved directly in the production process but helps the production process isell by raising the efficiency/ productivity level and reducing transaction costs. Services are intangible goods; they themselves cannot be seen but their effects can be seen. For example, services of a doctor cannot be seen, but its effect can be seen when patient gets cured and starts working, thus contributing to the production of output. In today's world, the most powerful economy is the one, which has a substantial share of the working population, engaged in the tertiary sector. Labour productivity is very much high in the tertiary sector thus leading to better emoluments of the workers present in the tertiary sector. One reason behind this is the higher skill levels of the workers of the tertiary sector. According to Kuznet, when the secondary expands along with the growth of GDP during the earlier stage of development of a developing economy, then income inequality starts rising.

Inter-sectoral analysis of an economy is interesting as it helps us to see the economy in terms of structural changes. In the input-output analysis, we basically try to see the linkages between various sectors and with the Gross Domestic Product (GDP). Inter-sectoral analysis becomes essential since all the sectors are not homogeneous and the input intensities vary across different sectors and there are sub-sectors too, within each sector Finally, centralised (socialistic) planning, mixed economic model/s, market based economic planning are just policy choices before any nation.

Ans. 8.
Safe driving habit Creating awareness is an important first step toward building audience understanding, influencing opinion and motivating behaviour. But there's a lot more than meets the eye to executing a successful awareness campaign and a lot more to it than enlisting the help of recognizable faces. Commanding audience attention is not as easy as it might appear.

Over-communication is a way of life. Information bombards the senses from every conceivable source, every waking moment of the day. Communication channels have mushroomed. Not only are there more choices within mediums, but also more mediums to choose from.

An effective media can raise the awareness level and can also bring about sustainable behavior change thereby reducing vulnerability to the Smoking Perils/Safe Driving Habit.

Media is capable of performing the following roles in preventing Smoking Perils/Safe Driving Habit.

A Channel for communication and Discussion: One of the roles of Media is to open the channels for communication and foster discussions about Smoking Perils/Safe Driving Habit and Addressing Smoking Perils/Safe Driving Habit in the entertainment programs can have an enormous impact on the society at risk.

A vehicle for Creating a supportive and enabling environment: Mass media can be instrumental in breaking the silence that envelopes the Smoking PERILS/Safe driving HABIT and in creating an encouraging behavior for combating with existing social norms and making positive changes in the society. Facilitator for removing Stigma and discriminations attached with the Smoking Perils/Safe Driving Habit.

A number of media campaigns have focused on the need to overcome prejudice and encourage solidarity with people who have given up such habits. A tool for creating a knowledge base for Smoking Perils/Safe Driving habit related services: The collaborative efforts of all modes of media in association with NGOs State organizations, service providers have brought to the lime light the availability and source of beneficial services like counselling, testing and other provisions, treatment and social care. The broadcasters and print media have a specific role to play as their efforts have tremendous recall value.

Education through entertainment: For creating an efficacious awareness about Smoking Perils/Safe Driving Habit, the messages need to be informative, educative as well as entertaining as these are mutually exclusive.

The education of Smoking Peril/Safe Driving Habit has to be spread as if we are selling the product. Thus, A holistic approach for dealing with the emotional, psychological and physical realities is to be adopted.

Mainstreaming: Broadcasters are mainstreaming the Smoking Peril/Safe Driving Habit issue across a number of programs, ensuring that the message permeates a diverse range of output, not just outlets and public service messages dedicated specifically to the issue. Putting Smoking Perils/Safe Driving Habit on the News agenda and encouraging leaders to participate: In recent years several leading broadcasters from around the world have found innovative ways to report on the subject.

Sharing resources ad pooling material: Several campaigns were successful as they fully utilized the opportunity of pooling the available resources with others by sharing expertise and material. Capacity Building: Successful partnerships need not be with other media outlets. Alliances of NGO, Government departments and foundations can bring significant benefit for both the parties.

Media as an institution of oversight, restraint and collaborative efforts: Media can render yeoman' service in providing accurate and correct news coverage of Smoking Perils/Safe Driving Habit facilitate eliciting and generating public response to state sponsored efforts. Such efforts have the potentials to awaken social and political leaders to review their strategies and take mid course corrections in regard to policy concerning Smoking Perils/Safe Driving Habit.

In such a process, the media has the potential to influence public opinion and attitudes about Smoking Perils/Safe Driving Habit Media too have the capability to bring about transformation in the thinking pattern of the society and thus sowing the seeds of attitudinal changes. The media can be a great facilitator for preventing process while imparting the need for a healthy behaviour towards the section of the society and those individuals most vulnerable to Smoking Perils/Safe Driving Habit and those individuals affected by it.

Ans. 9.
It is difficult to answer whether products do need packaging, or the consumer does?
For whom is the package made? The product, or the consumer? The package is tailor-made for the product, but one shall not forget that all the products are made for consumers.
From the consumer's point of view the package's function is to protect the product. In the case of bulk goods, or if the product cannot be used without the support of the package, the packages must help the use of the product. Without the service of packaging, most of the goods, especially food, couldn't reach the consumer. Living in the countryside, one can buy goods, for example milk directly from the farmer, but a can is needed to carry it home. This can also be considered as a refillable package , with almost an unlimited number of uses. In a city, milk can only be bought from the store, packed in aseptic carton box. It is rnot possible to avoid it, unless one goes daily to the dairy, and drink from the tap.
From the packager's point of view, the most important function of the packaging is the protection of the usage and aesthetic values of the product from damages, and get the product sold to the consumer. For the producer, the package is also a value-creating media of the product. With the help of the package, the product can be sold to the consumer. For example, a barrel full of toothpaste has almost no purchase value, since who wants to buy 100 litre of toothpaste? Most probably nobody would buy even a handful of it in the grocery, but one certainly does buy 50 grams of toothpaste in a tube.

Modern packaging's are an expressive form of the consumer-lifestyle. Over the protective function, packaging's are giving character, "personality" to the product. They are following the product to the consumer, giving practical as well as aesthetic value. The proportion of the usage and aesthetic functions is important. The quality of packaging reflects our universal culture. All those products that appear in the shops and offer themselves for purchase, apart of that- with very few exceptions- their usage function is primary, are creating the surrounding material environment.

Primary packaging is the material the first envelops the product and holds it. Secondary packaging is outside the primary packaging – perhaps used to group primary packaging together.

Role of Packaging

The role of packaging is containment, protection, safety, and display. If you are selling your product through retail stores, you are trying to use your packaging to:
- Catch the browsers attention
- Create desire
- Inspire confidence

What is the Importance of Packaging?

The Importance of Packaging Let's talk about packaging. Packaging can be thought about in many different ways, but if we think purely about the purpose of packaging first, we find the purpose is to: Contain the product Communicate product information Facilitate product storage and shipment Reinforce branding.

Packaging is important, but you need to determine how critical it is based on your marketing/distribution methods.

The packaging is a type of advertisement - even if it goes through mail order to the customer's shelf for peers to see. These peers are potential customers - and most likely they will have the same needs as the person who already made the purchase. The package becomes even more critical if you plan to distribute your product through resellers and it will sit on a shelf in a store. There is à lot of competition for the customer's attention. If you plan to do this, it is probably best to get a graphic designer to help you.

Use descriptive titles for the product- not necessarily creative. Many people go into a retail store looking for products to perform a function, but don't necessarily have a specific product in mind. You need to communicate your function and benefits to them quickly and effectively. Graphics and slogans on the package should reflect the usage of the product. Avoid technical jargon except for declaring content requirements. Resellers are a good source of information for good packaging design. Ask for a reseller's input on a design.

Include testimonial from existing users. This will inspire confidence. Include a sales literature in your packaging for the customer to pass on to their colleagues.

Stickers on a package work very well for attracting attention. In addition, you can use them to your advantage.

Ans. 10.

Police organizations collect and store a vast amount of information. Traditionelly, this information resided on sheets of paper stored in file cabinets. Today, police organizations are being transformed by the information age. Most have implemented management information systems (MIS) to record, store, access, and analyze data on calls-for-service from citizens, the nature of the police response to these calls, reported crimes, arrests, gun permits, motor vehicle stops and many other types of data. Some agencies maintain centralized control over access to information, while others have adopted integrated management systems that can be accessed by law enforcement officials at any level(from patrol officer to chief). This "all access" approach allows employees with different needs to access the data without having to wait or file a formal request. Some agencies store and access data electronically, but do not use it as a means for improving the organization. Others use data as a tool to improve management and operations. While most large police agencies today have made enormous improvements in their capacity to collect and store large amounts of data, many have made little progress in using the data they collect. Developing the ability to use data for improving operations and management represents an important challenge for police organizations today. This section introduces some of the information technologies used by police and discusses their potential for improving police management.

Computer Aided Dispatch systems (CAD) are now commonly used by many police departments. CAD systems prioritize calls-for-service received by the communications center, "stacking" less urgent calls so that police officers can respond to those calls requiring more immediate attention. Once a call is prioritized by the CAD system, it can be broadcast to an officer in a patrol car through either the radio or a computer. CAD makes it easier for human calltakers and dispatchers to remain abreast of what calls are being answered, where officers are located, and how long they have been out on a call. This reduces the likelihood of dispatching errors and enhances officer safety (George). CAD systems are also useful for collecting and storing data. Once a call is received at the communications center, it is categorized by the CAD system. Depending on the agency's information storage capacity, the data are then integrated into the information system for some period of time, after which they are archived for long-ternm storage.

Many police agencies in the United States now have Mobile Digital Terminals(MDTS) or Computers (MDCS) installed in their patrol cars (hereafter referred to as MDTS). MDTS have a number of uses, not all of which are available in all jurisdictions. First, they allow an officer to receive "silent dispatches" over the computer rather than through the radio, so that police scanners can not be used to monitor police communications. Second, officers can check motor vehicle registrations, drivers' licenses, and outstanding warrants directly, without having to wait for a dispatcher to run a computer check. Third, officers can enter police reports into the computer while out in the field, rather than having to return to the police station early to complete paperwork. Fourth, officers can send e-mail to other officers, including those who are not on duty at the time. Finally, officers can sometimes retrieve information on arrests,

criminal backgrounds, and calls for service from databases that are networked between agencies at local, state, or federal levels. According to the 1997 Law Enforcement Management and Administrative Statistics (LEMAS) survey, 78 percent of large municipal law enforcement agencies in the United States use some type of mobile digital terminal or computer (Reaves and Gold berg).

Ans. 11.

Typically, the phrase "organizational change" is about a significant change in the organization, such as reorganization or adding a major new product or service. This is in contrast to smaller changes, such as adopting a new computer procedure. Organizational change can seem like such a vague phenomena that it is helpful if you can think of change in terms of various dimensions as described below.

Organization-wide Versus Subsystem Change

Examples of organization- wide change might be a major restructuring, collaboration or "rightsizing." Usually, organizations must undertake organization-wide change to evolve to a different level in their life cycle, for example, going from a highly reactive, entrepreneurial organization to one that has a more stable and planned development.

Experts assert that successful organizational change requires a change in culture-cultural change is another example of organization-wide change. Examples of a change in a subsystem might include addition or removal of a product or service, reorganization of a certain department, or implementation of a new process to deliver products or services.

Transformational Versus Incremental Change

An example of transformational (or radical, fundamental) change might be changing an organization's structure and culture from the traditional top-down, hierarchical structure to a large amount of self-directing teams. Another example might be Business Process Re-engineering, which tries to take apart (at least on paper, at first) the major parts and processes of the organization and then put them back together in a more optimal fashion. Transformational change is sometimes referred to as quantum change. Examples of incremental change might include continuous improvement as a quality management process or implementation of new computer system to increase efficiencies. Many times, organizations experience incremental change and its leaders do not recognize the change as such.

Remedial Versus Developmental Change

Change can be intended to remedy current situations, for example, to imnprove the poor performance of a product on the entire organization, reduce burnout in the workplace, help the organization to become much more proactive and less reactive, or address large budget deficits. Remedial projects often seem more focused and urgent because they are addressing a current, major problem. It is often easier to determine the success of these projects because the problem is solved or not. Change can also be developmental to make a successful situation even more successful, for example, expand the amount of customers served, or duplicate successful products or services. Developmental projects can seem more general and vague than remedial, depending on how specific goals are and how important it is for members of the organization to achieve those goals. Some people might have different perceptions of what is a remedial change versus a developmental change. They might see that if developmental changes are not made soon, there will be need for remedial changes. Also, organizations may recognize current remedial issues and then establish a developmental vision to address the issues. In those situations, projects are still remedial because they were conducted primarily to address current issues.

<u>Unplanned Versus Planned Change</u>

Unplanned change usually occurs because of a major, sudden surprise to the organization, which causes its members to respond in a highly reactive and disorganized fashion. Unplanned change might occur when the Chief Executive

Officer suddenly leaves the organization, significant public relations problems occur, poor product performance quickly results in loss of customers, or other disruptive situations arise. Planned change occurs when leaders in the organization recognize the need for a major change and proactively organize a plan to accomplish the change.

Planned change occurs with successful implementation of a Strategic Plan, plan for reorganization, or other implementation of a change of this magnitude. Note that planned change, even though based on a proactive and well-done plan, often does not occur in a highly organized fashion. Instead, planned change tends to occur in more of a chaotic and disruptive fashion than expected by participants.

Ans. 12.

A chi-square test (also chi-squared or 2 test) is any statistical hypothesis test in which the test statistic has a chi-square distribution when the null hypothesis is true, or any in which the probability distribution of the test statistic (assuming the null hypothesis is true) can be made to approximate a chi-square distribution as closely as desired by
making the sample size large enough.

Some examples of chi-squared tests where the chi-square distribution is only approximately valid:

- Pearson's chi-square test, also known as the chi-square goodness-of-fit test or chi-square test for independence. When mentioned without any modifiers or without other precluding context, this test is usually understood.
- Yates' chi-square test, also known as Yates correction for continuity.
- Mantel-Haens zel chi-square test.
- Linear-by-linear association chi-square test.
- The portmanteau test in time-series analysis, testing for the presence of autocorrelation.
- Likelihood-ratio tests in general statistical modelling. for testing whether there is evidence of the need to move from a simple model to a more complicated one (where the simple model is nested within the complicated one).

One case where the distribution of the test statistic is an exact chi-square distribution is the test that the variance of a normally-distributed population has a given value based on a sample variance. Such a test is uncommon in practice because values of variances to test against are seldom known exactly

Chi-square test

The chi-square is one of the most popular statistics because it is easy to calculate and interpret. There are two kinds of chi-square tests. The first is called a one-way analysis, and the second is called a two-way analysis. The purpose of both is to determine whether the observed frequencies (counts) markedly differ from the frequencies that we would expect by chance.

The observed cell frequencies are organized in rows and columns like a spreadshect. This table of observed cell frequencies is called a contingency table, and the chi-square test if part of a contingency table analysis.

The chi-square statistic is the sum of the contributions from each of the individual cells. Every cell in a table contributes something to the overall chi-square statistic. If a given cell difters markedly from the expected frequency, then the contribution of that cell to the overall chi-square is large. If a cell is close to the expected frequery for that cell, then the contribution of that cell to the overall chi-square is low. A large chi-square statistic indicates that somewhere in the table, the observed frequencies differ markedly from the expected frequencies It does rot tell which cell (or cells) are causing the high chi-square...only that they are there. When a chi-square is high, you must visually examine the table to determine which cell(s) are responsible.

When there are exactly two rows and two columns, the chi-square statistic becomes inaccurate, and Yate's correction for continuity is usually applied. Statistics Calculator will automatically use Yate's correction for two by-two tables when the expected frequency of any cell is less than 5 or the total N is less than 50.

If there is only one column or one row (a one-way chi-square test), the degrees of freedom is the number of cells minus one. For a two way chi-square, the degrees of freedom is the number or rows minus one times the number of columns minus one.

Using the chi-square statistic and its associated degrees of freedom, the software reports the probability that the differences between the observed and expected frequencies occurred by chance. Generally, a probability of .05 or less is considered to be a significant difference.

A standard spreadsheet interface is used to enter the counts for each cell. After you've finished entering the data, the program will print the chi-square, degrees of freedom and probability of chance.

Use caution when interpreting the chi-square statistic if any of the expected cell frequencies are less than five. Also, use caution when the total for all cells is less than 50.

Example: A drug manufacturing company conducted a survey of customers. The research question is : Is there a significant relationship between packaging preference (size of the bottle purchased) and economic status? There were four packaging sizes: small, medium, large, and jumbo. Economic status was: lower, middle, and upper. The following data was collected.

	Lower	Middle	Upper
Small	24	22	18
Medium	23	28	19
Large	18	27	29
Jumbo	16	21	23

Chi-square statistic = 9.743
Degrees o freedom = 6
Probability of chance = .1359
Fisher's exact test
The chi-square statistic becomes inaccurate when used to analyze contingency tables that contain exactly two rows and two columns, and that contain less than 50 cases. Fisher's exact probability is not plagued by inaccuracies due to Small N's. Therefore, it should be used for two-by-two contingency tables that contain fewer than 50 cases.
Example
Here are the results of a public opinion poll broken down by gender. What is the exact probability that the difference between the observed and expected frequencies ccurred by chance?

	Male	Female
Favor	10	14
Opposed	15	9

Fisher's exact probability = . 0828
Binomial test
The binomial distribution is used for calculating the probability of dichotomous outcomes in which the two choices are mutually exclusive. The program requires that you enter the number of trials, probability of the desired outcome on each trial, end the number of times the desired outcome was observed.

Example:
If we were to flip a coin one hundred times, and it came up heads seventy times, what is the probability of this happening?
Number of trials: 100
Probability of success on each trial (0-1): 5
Number of successes: 70
Probability of 70 or more successes < .0001

Poisson distribution events test
The poissen distribution, like the binomial distribution, is used to determine the probability of an observed frequency. It is used to describe the number of events that will occur in a specific period of time or in a specific area or volume. You need to enter the observed and expected frequencies.

Example:
Previous research on a particular assembly line has shown that they have an average daily defect rate of 39 products. Thus, the expected number of defective products expected on any day is 39. The day after implementing a new quality control program, they found only 25 defects. What is the probability of seeing 25 or fewer defects on any day?
Observed frequency: 25
Expected frequency: 39
Probability of 25 or fewer events = . 0226

Ans. 13.
Traditional Economics is- The social science that deals with the production, distribution, and consumption of goods and services and with the theory and management of economies or economic systems. The foundations of TRADITIONAL economics and all the social sciences has multiple fundamental flaws which includes an intrinsic inconsistency in utility theory. In game theory undefined sums are used to define basic concepts, the characteristic function is ill-defined, and there are other fundamental errors. In measurement theory the models of even the most elementary variables such as length and mass are incorrect, and in decision theory even what is being measured is not understood. These errors must be removed explained and their correction outlined. Correcting these theories will lead to better decisions by individuals, organizations, affecting everyday lives of people throughout the world.
In Business, Management Decision making Needs

Steps of Structured Decision Making:
- Problem definition: What specific decision has to be made? What are the spatial and temporal scope of the decision? Will the decision be iterated over time?
- Objectives: What are the management objectives? Ideally, these are stated in quantitative terms that relate to metrics that can be measured. Setting objectives falls in the realm of policy, and should be informed by legal and regulatory mandates, as well as stakeholder viewpoints. A number of methods for stakeholder elicitation
and conflict resolution are appropriate for clarifying objectives.
- Alternatives: What are the different management actions to choose from? This element requires explicit articulation of the alternatives available to the decision maker. The range of permissible options is often constrained by legal or political considerations, but structured assessment may lead to creative new alternatives.
- Consequences: What are the consequences of different management actions? How much of the objectives would each alternative achieve? In structured decision-making, we predict the consequences of the alternative actions with some type of model Depending on the information available or the quantification desired for a structured decision process consequences may be modeled with highly scientific computer applications or with personal judgment elicited carefully and transparently. Ideally, models are quantitative, but they need not be; the important thing is that they link actions to consequences.
- Tradeoffs: If there are multiple objectives, how do they trade off with each ather? In most complex decisions, the best we can do is choose intelligently between less-than perfect alternatives. Numerous tools are available to help determine the relative importance or weights among conflicting objectives and to then compare alternatives across multiple attributes to find the 'best' compromise solutions.
- Uncertainty: Because we rarely know precisely how management actions will affect natural systems, decisions are frequently made in the face of uncertainty. Uncertainty makes choosing among alternative far more difficult. A good decision-making process will

confront uncertainty explicitly, and evaluate the likelihood of different outcomes and their possible consequences.
- Risk Tolerance: Identifying the uncertainty that impedes decision-making, then analyzing the risk that uncertainty presents to management is an important step in making a good decision. Understanding the level of risk a decision-maker is willing to accept, or the risk response determined by law or policy, will make the decision-making process more objectives-driven, transparent, and defensible.
- Linked decisions: Many important decisions are linked over time. The key to dealing effectively with linked decisions is to isolate and resolve the near-term issues while sequencing the collection of information needed for future decisions

To Make Such Structured Decisions with the Help of "Traditional Economics" is not Feasible.

Hence, here we make use of the Managerial Economics.

Managerial economics (also called business economics), is a branch of economics that applies microeconomic analysis to specific business decisions. As such, it bridges economic theory and economics in practice. It draws heavily from quantitative techniques such as regression analysis and correlation, Lagrangian calculus (linear). If there is a unifying theme that runs through most of managerial economics it is the attempt to optimize business decisions given the firm's objectives and given constraints imposed by scarcity, for example through the use of operations research and programming.

"Managerial economics is the application of economic principles and methodologies to the decision-making process within the firm or organization."

"Managerial economics applies economic theory and methods to business and administrative decision-making."

"Managerial economics refers to the application of economic theory and the tools of analysis of decision science to examine how an organisation can achieve its objectives most effectively."

"It is the application of economic analysis to business problems; it has its origin in theoretical microeconomics."

Managerial Model M Building

The steps: the hypothetical-deductive approach make assumptions about behaviour work out the consequences of those assumptions make predictions test the predictions against the evidence Predictions Supported? The model is accepted as a good explanation (for the moment) Predictions Refuted? Go back and re-work the whole process

Should Assumptions be Realistic?

The assumption of profit-maximising may be unrealistic or inaccurate However, what matters is the explanatory or predictive power of a theory (or model), not the descriptive realism of its assumptions. A model built on unrealistic assumptions may give good predictions. Assumptions are a necessary simplifying device

Example: Overtaking

What Is A "Good" Model?

It allows us to make predictions and set hypotheses

The predictions can be tested against the empirical evidence

The predictions are supported by the empirical evidence

Managerial Economics

Economics in general takes a positive and predictive appreach not prescriptive or 'normative' trying to explain "what is" not what "should be" the main objective is to understand how a market economy works Not very concerned about the descriptive realism of assumptions: "I assume X" does not mean "I believe X to be true" Some real tension if the models are used for prescription assume "perfect knowledge: OK for model-building cannot say to a manager: "behave AS IF you had perfect knowledge".

Ans. 14

The degree to which a demand or supply curve reacts to a change in price is the curve's Elasticity. Elasticity varies among products because some products may be more essential to the consumer. Products that are necessities are more insensitive to price changes because consumers would continue buying these products despite price increases. Conversely, a price increase of a good or service that is considered less of a necessity will deter more consumers because the opportunity cost of buying the product will become too high.

A good or service is considered to be highly elastic if a slight change in price leads to a sharp change in the quantity demanded or supplied. Usually these kinds of products are readily available in the market and a person may not necessarily need them in his or her daily life. On the other hand, an inelastic good or service is one in which changes in price witness only modest changes in the quantity demanded or supplied, if any at all. These goods tend to be things that are more of a necessity to the consumer in his or her daily life.

To determine the elasticity of the Supply or Demand curves, we can use this simple equation:

Elasticity (% change in quantity/% change in price)

If elasticity is greater than or equal to one, the curve is considered to be elastic. If it is less than one, the curve is said to be inelastic.

As we mentioned previously, the demand curve is a negative slope, and if there is a large decrease in the quantity demanded with a small increase in price, the demand curve looks flatter, or more horizontal. This flatter curve means that the good or service in question is elastic.

Meanwhile, inelastic demand is represented with a much more upright curve as quantity changes little with a large movement in price.

Elasticity of supply works similarly If a change in price results in a big change in the amount supplied, the supply curve appears flatter and is considered elastic. Elasticity in this case would be greater than or equal to one.

On the other hand, if a big change in price only results in a minor change in the quantity supplied, the supply curve is steeper and its elasticily would be less than one. Factors Affecting Demand Elasticity.

There are three main factors that influence a demand's price elasticity:
1. The availability of substitutes: This is probably the most important lactor influencing the elasticity of a good or service. In general, the more substitutes, the more elastic the demand will be. For example, if the price of a cup of coffee increases consumers could replace their morning caffeine with a cup of tea. This means that coffee is an elastic good because a raise in price will cause a large decrease in demand as consumers start buying more tea instead of coffee.
However, if the price of caffeine were to go up as a whole, we would probably see little change in the consumption of coffee or tea because there are few substitutes for
caffeine. Most people are not willing to give up their morning cup of cafleine no matter what the price. We would say, therefore, that caffeine is an inelastic product because of its lack of substitutes. Thus, while a product within an industry is elastic due to the availability of substitutes, the industry itself tends to be inelastic. Usually, unique goods such as diamonds are inelastic because they have few if any substitutes.
2. Amount of income available to spend on the good: This factor affecting demand elasticity refers to the total a person can spend on a particular good or service. Thus, if the price of a can of Coke increases and income stays the same, the income that is available to spend on coke, which is now enough for only two rather than four cans-
of Coke. In other words, the consumer is forced to reduce his or her demand of Coke. Thus if there is an increase in price and no change in the amount of income available to spend on the good, there will be an elastic reaction in demand, demand will be sensitive to a change in price if there is no change in income.
3. Time: The third influential factor is time. If the price of cigarettes increases, a smoker with very few available substitutes will most likely continue buying his or her daily cigarettes. This means that tobacco is inelastic because the change in price will not have a significant influence on the quantity demanded. However, if that smoker finds that he or she cannot afford to spend the extra amount per day and begins to kick the habit over a period of time, the price elasticity of cigarettes for that consumer becomes elastic in the long run.

Price elasticity of demand is defined as the measure of responsiveness in the quantity demanded for a commodity as result of change in price of the same commodity. In other words, it is percentage change in quantity demanded as per the percentage change in price of the same commodity. In economics and business studies, the price elasticity of demand (PED) is a measure of the sensitivity of quantity demanded to changes in price. It is measured as elasticity, that is it measures the relationship as the ratio of percentage changes between quantity demanded of a good and changes in its price. Drinking water is a good example of a good that has inelastic characteristics in that people will pay anything for it (high or low prices with relatively equivalent quantity demanded), so it is not elastic. On the other hand demand for sugar is very elastic because as the price of sugar increases, there are many substitutions which
consumers may switch to. A price drop usually results in an increase in the quantity demanded by consumers. The demand for a good is relatively inelastic when the change in quantity demanded is less than change in price. Goods and services for which no substitutes exist are generally inelastic. Demand for an antibiotic, for example, becomes highly inelastic when it alone can kill an infection resistant to all other antibiotics. Rather than die of an infection, patients will generally be willing to pay whatever is necessary to acquire enough of the antibiotic to kill the infection. A number of factors determine the elasticity:

Substitutes: The more substitutes, the higher the elasticity, as people can easily switch from one good to another if a minor price change is made
- Percentnge of income: The higher the percentage that the product's price is of the consumers income, the higher the elasticity, as people will be careful with purchasing the good because of its cost
- Necessity: The more necessary a good is, the lower the elasticity, as people will attempt to buy it no matter the price, such as the case of insulin for those that need it.
- Duration: The longer a price change holds, the higher the elasticity, as more and more people will stop demanding the goods (i.e. if you go to the supermarket and find that blueberries have doubled in price, you'll buy it because you need it this time, but next time you won't, unless the price drops back down again)

Breadth of definition: The broader the definition, the lower the elasticity. For exaumple, Company X's fried dumplings will have a relatively high elasticity, where as food in general will have an extremely low elasticity (see Substitutes, Necessity above) Substitute good In economics, one kind of good (or service) is said to be a substitute good for another kind in so far as the two kinds of goods can be consumed or used in place of one another in at least some of their possible uses.

Examples: Classic examples of substitute goods include margarine and butter, or petroleum and natural gas (used for heating or electricity). The fact that one good is substitutable for another has immediate economic consequences different types.

It is important to note that when speaking about substitute goods we are speaking about two different kinds of goods, so the "substitutability" of one good for another is always a matter of degree. One good is a perfect substitute for another only if it can be used in exactly the same way. In that case the utility of a combination is an increasing function of the sum of the two amounts, and theoretically, in the case of a price difference, there would be no demand for the more expensive good.

Perfect and Imperfect substitutes.

Perfect substitutes may alternately be characterized as goods having a constant marginal rate of substitution. Alternate types of soft drinks are commonly used as an example of perfect substitutes. As the price of Coca Cola rises, consumers would be expected to substitute Pepsi in equal quantities, i.e., total cola consumption would hold constant. Also, blank media such as a writable Compact Discs from alternate manufacturers would be perfect substitutes. If one manufacturer raises the price of its CDs, consumers would be expected to switch to a lower cost manufacturer. Imperfect substitutes exhibit variable marginal rates of a substitution along the consumer indifference curve.

Perfect Competition One of the requirements for perfect competition is that the products of competing firms should be perfect substitutes. When this condition is not satisfied, the market is characterized by product differentiation. Good Substitution Substitute goods exhibit no complementarities, as in a complementary good. In other words, good substitution is an economic concept where two goods are of comparable value. Car brands are an example. While someone could argue that Ford trucks are considerably different from Toyota trucks, if the price of Ford trucks goes up enough, some people will buy Toyota trucks instead.

Ans. 15.

Oligopoly.

A market structure characterized by a small number of large firms that dominate the market, selling either identical or differentiated products, with significant barriers to entry into the industry. This is one of four basic market structures. The other three are perfect competition, monopoly, and monopolistic competition. Oligopoly dominates the modern economic landscape, accounting for about half of all output produced in the economy. Oligopolistic industries are as diverse as they are widespread, ranging from breakfast cereal to cars, from computers to aircraft, from television broadcasting to pharmaceuticals, from petroleum to detergent.

Oligopoly is a market structure characterized by a small number of relatively large firms that dominate an industry. The market can be dominated by as few as two firms or as many as twenty, and still be considered oligopoly. With fewer than two firms, the industry is monopoly. As the number of firms increase (but with no exact number) oligopoly becomes monopolistic competition.

Because an oligopolistic firm is relatively large compared to the overall market, it has a substantial degree of market control. It does not have the total control over the supply side as exhibited by monopoly, but its capital is significantly greater than that of a monopolistically competitive firm.

Relative size and extent of market control means that interdependence among firms in an industry is a key feature of oligopoly. The actions of one firm depend on and influence the actions of another. Such interdependence creates a number of interesting economic issues. One is the tendency for competing oligopolistic firms to turn into cooperating oligopolistic firms. When they do, inefficiency worsens, and they tend to come under the scrutiny of government. Alternatively, oligopolistic firms tend to be a prime source of innovations, innovations that promote technological advances and economic growth. Like much of the imperfection that makes up the real world, there is both good and bad with oligopoly. The challenge in economics is, of course, to promote the good and limit the bad.

The three most important characteristics of oligopoly are:
1. an industry dominated by a small number of large firms,
2. firms sell either identical or differentiated products, and
3. the industry has significant barriers to entry.

Let us discuss each of the above in detail:
- **Small Number of Large Firms:** An oligopolistic industry is dominated by a small number of large firms, each of which is relatively large compared to the overall size of the market. This generates substantial market control, the extent of market control depending on the number and size of the firms.
- **Identical or Differentiated Products:** Some oligopolistic industries produce identical products, while others produce differentiated products. Identical product oligopolies tend to process raw materials or intermediate goods that are used as inputs by other industries. Notable examples are petroleum, steel, and aluminium. Differentiated product oligopolies tend to focus on consumer goods that satisfy the wide variety of consumer wants and needs.

A few examples of differentiated oligopolistic industries include automobiles, household detergents, and computers.

Barriers to Entry: Firms in a oligopolistic industry attain and retain market control through barriers to entry. The most common barriers to entry include patents, resource ownership, government franchises, start-up cost, brand name recognition, and decreasing average cost. Each of these make it extremely difficult, if not impossible,

for potential firms to enter an industry. Behavior Although oligopolistic industries tend to be diverse, they also tend to exhibit several behavioral tendencies:

(i) interdependence,
(ii) rigid prices.
(iii) nonprice competition,
(iv) mergers, and
(v) Collusion Interdependence Each oligopolistic firm keeps a close eye on the activities of other firms in the industry. Decisions made by one firm invariably affect others and are invariably affected by others and are invariably affected by others. Competition among interdependent oligopoly firms is comparable to a game or an athletic contest. One team's success depends not only on its own actions but on the actions of its competitor. Oligopolistic firms engage in competition among the few.

Ans. 16.

Types of Organization Design/Structure

1. Horizontal Organization

   Horizontal organizations consist of teams which are organized around business processes and which are responsible for the results they generate. By flattening portions of the organization and holding the team members accountable for results, it asserts that decisions will be made more quickly and more consistently with business objectives. This tool seeks to reduce problems with cross-functional coordination by ensuring that the team members have the necessary skills to have end-to-end accountability far the process.

Approach

The following steps are critical to creating a horizontal organization:
- Horizontal teams around the most critical business processes.
- Give team members ownership of the process and assign a clear process leader.
- Cross-train team members for the range of skills needed for their process.
- Tie performance measures directly to customer requirements for the process, and reward individuals for individual and team contributions.
- Create career development paths consistent with developing team consistent with developing team skills.
- Redefine managers' roles to focus on enabling teams to perform through training, coaching, sharing, information, and setting strategic direction.
- Benefits

  Horizontal organizations are often used to structure processes which requires extensive crossfunctional coordination. This tool increases the responsiveness and productivity of an organization. Additionally, horizontal organizations can be used to balance local and global needs within a multinational corporation by creating a network linking the desparate operations.

1. Virtual Organization

   A virtual organization or company is one whose members are geographically apart, usually working by computer EMAIL and

GROUPWARE while appearing to others to be a single, unified organization with a real physical location.

Steps to a Virtual Organization

Outsourcing mainly to reduce costs where there is some experience in working at a distance, but three is one dominant party and high certainty of what everyone must do.

Forming strategic alliances to share the work and gain experience in developing and sharing common goals. Here there is no dominant party although the parties are fixed. and then becoming virtual organizations to achieve flexibility. Now the partners themselves can quickly change, with greater emphasis on the use of knowledge to create new and innovative products.

2. Inverted Pyramid

Many of today's leaders view their organization as a pyramid,, with senior leadership atop the apex, disseminating orders and snapping the proverbial finger expecting immediate respanses. Below him or her reside lower echelon leaders and workers organized in subordinate tiers.

This construct is irrespective of your organization's size. If you want to succeed you need to get to the top. Your organization then succeeds because you pulled them to victory. This perception of leadership has been the norm in nearly every military, governmental and civilian organization.

Matrix Structure

Different structures can be combined together. When one has two parallel organizational structures this is called a matrix structure. The idea is to combine the advantages of two structures, but this has the obvious disadvantage of being harder to coordinate and introducing more potential conflict. In the past most large companies were centralized-that is, involved structures in which decisions were taken at the centre or upper levels of organization. Just as there has been a move to flatter organizations, so there has been a move to decentralized ones.

Characteristics

- Reinforces & broadens technical excellence
- Facilitates efficient use of resources
- Balances conflicting objectives of the organization
- Increases power conflicts

- Increases confusion & stress for 2-boss employees
- Impedes decision making

Mechanistic Organization

Mechanistic organizations are often appropriate in stable environments and for routine tasks and technologies. In some ways similar to burcaucratic structures, mechanistic organizations have clear, well-defined, centralized, vertical hierarchies of command, authority, and control. Efficiency and predictability are emphasized through specialization, standardization, and formalization. This results in rigidly defined jobs,

technologies, and processes. The term mechanistic suggests that organizational structures, processes, and roles are like a machine in which each part of the organization does what it is designed to do, but little else.

Ans. 17.

Job design refers to the way that a set of tasks, or an entire job, is organized. Job design helps to determine:

What tasks are done, how the tasks are done, how many tasks are done, and in what order the tasks are done. It takes into account all factors which affect the work, and organizes the content and tasks so that the whole job is less likely to be a risk to the employee. Job design involves administrative areas such as:

Job rotation, job enlargement, task/machine pacing, work breaks, and working hours. A well designed job will encourage a variety of 'good' body positions, have reasonable strength requirements, require a reasonable amount of mental activity, and help foster feelings of achievement and self-esteem.

How can job design help with the organization of work?

Job design principles can address problems such as: work overload, work under load, repetitiveness, limited control over work, isolation, shift work, delays in filling vacant positions, excessive working hours, and limited understanding of the whole job process. Job design is sometimes considered as a way to help deal with stress in the workplace.

Is there a difference between job design and workplace design?

Job design and workplace design are often used interchangeably because both contribute to keep the physical requirements of a job reasonable. Job design refers to administrative changes that can help improve working conditions. In comparison, workplace design concentrates on dealing with the workstation, the tools, and the body position that all influence the way a person does his or her work. Good workplace design reduces static positions, repetitive motions and awkward body positions.

What are features of "good" job design?

Good job design accommodates employees' mental and physical characteristics by paying attention to: muscular energy such as work/rest schedules or pace of work, and mental energy such as boring versus extremely difficult tasks.

What are common approaches to job design?

Achieving good job design involves administrative practices that determine what the employee does, for how long. where, and when as well as giving the employees choice where ever possible. In job design, you may choose to examine the various tasks of an individual job or the design of a group of jobs.

Approaches to job design include:

Job Enlargement: Job enlargement changes the jobs to include more and/or different tasks. Job enlargement should add interest to the work but may or may not give employees more responsibility.

Job Rotation: Job rotation moves employees from one task to another. It distributes the group tasks among a number of employees.

Job Enrichment: Job enrichment allows employees to assume more responsibility, accountability, and independence when learning new tasks or to allow tor greater participation and new opportunities.

Work Design (Job Engineering): Work design allows employees to see how the work methods, layout and handling procedures link together as well as the interaction between people and machines.

Before a Job Design is Done, a Job Analysis Should be Carried Out.

Job Analysis is a process to identify and determine in detail the particular job duties and requirements and the relative importance of these duties for a given job. Job Analysis is a process where judgements are made about data collected on a job.

There are two key elements of a job analysis:

1. Identification of major job requirements (MJRS) which are the most important duties and responsibilities of the position to be filled. They are the main purpose or primary reasons the position exists. The primary source of MJRS is the most current, official position description.

2. Identification of knowledge, skills and abilities (KSAS) required to accomplish each MJR and the quality level and amount of the KSAS needed. Most job analyses deal with KSAS that are measurable, that can be documented, and produce meaningful differences between candidates. Typically, possession of KSAS is demonstrated by experience, education, or training. The goal of KSAS is to identify those candidates who are potentially best qualified to perform the position to be filled; they are most useful when they provide meaningful distinctions among qualified candidates. Source documents for KSAS may be the position description, HRM standard qualifications and job classification standards.

Job Analysis should collect information on the following areas:

Duties and Tasks: The basic unit of a job is the performance of specific tasks and duties. Information to be collected about these items may include: frequency, duration, effort, skill, complexity, equipment standards, etc

Environment: This may have a significant impact on the physical requirements to be able to perform a job. The work environment may include unpleasant conditions such as offensive odors and temperature extremes. There may also be definite risks to the incumbent such as noxious fumes, radioactive substances, hostile and aggressive people, and dangerous explosives.

Tools and Equipment: Some duties and tasks are performed using specific equipment and tools. Equipment may include protective clothing. These items need to be specified in a Job Analysis.

Relationships: Supervision given and received. Relationships with internal or external people.

Requirements: The knowledges, skills, and abilities (KSA's) required to perform the job. While an incumbent may have higher KSA's than those required for the job, a Job Analysis typically only states the minimum requirements to perform the job.

Approaches to Job Design using Socio Technical Systems

There are three important approaches to job design, viz, Engineering approach, Human approach and The Job characteristic approach.

Engineering Approach: The most important single element in the Engineering approaches, proposed by FW Taylor and others, was the task idea, "The work of every workman is fully planned out by the management at least one day in advance and each man receives in most cases complete written instructions, describing in detail the ask which he is to accomplish.

This task specifies not only what is to be done but how it is to be done and the exact time allowed for doing it."

The principles offered by scientific management to job design can be summarized thus:

1. Work should be scientifically studied.
2. Work should be arranged so that workers can be efficient.
3. Employees selected for work should be matched to the demands of the job.
4. Employees should be trained to perform the job.
5. Monetary compensation should be used to reward successful performance of the job.

These principles to job design seem to be quite rational and appealing because they point towards increased organizational performance. Specialization and reutilization over a period of time result in job incumbents becoming experts rather quickly, leading to higher levels of output. Despite the assumed gains in efficiency, behavioural scientists have found that some job incumbents dislike specialised and routine jobs.

Ans. 18.

Organizational Diagnosis

Organizational Diagnosis helps organizations identify the "gaps" between "what is" and "what ought to be." Once we gain a shared vision of the desired state, we identify barriers and work toward solutions.

The Six-Phase approach to organizational diagnosis is tailored to the specific needs of each co:

Phase 1: Define develop a shared understanding of the task, issue, or problem along with a for diagnosis.

Phase 2: Diagnose examine organizational archival reports/documents and utilize information gathered through interviews, focus groups, questionnaires & surveys, along with objective observations lo collect relevant data.

Phase 3: Analyze After collecting the data, use statistical analysis methods to interpret the data and develop practical recommendations.

Phase 4: Presentation of Findings This phase involves determining an effective intervention strategy.

Phase 5: Action Planning We work with key players from the organization to develop an action plan that: Fits the needs of the organization Will yield measurable results Will enhance the organization's capacity to manage change Is catered to the organization's situation, culture, context, and maturational cycle.

Phase 6: Reinforce maintaining a focus on the desired state and helping organizations sustain change initiatives. The reinforce phase ensures effective implementation of our action plan and outlines the next steps to take once the action plan has been implemented.

Organization analysis is the second stage, where we analyze the information a scientific manner and develop a strategy/action plan. The organizational analysis include:

1. **Environmental Analysis:** Environmental analysis is defined as the process by which strategists monitor the economic, governmental, legal, market, competitive, supplier, technological, geographic, and social cultural settings to determine opportunities and threats to their firms/company/organization. Environment diagnosis principally consists of managerial decisions made by strategist for analyzing the significance of the data like Strengths, weakness, opportunities and threats of the organization to has to design their own strategy for formulation, implementation and controlling the internal environmental factors.

   Environmental analysis helps to strategic executive and manager to diagnosis of strategic competitive force and components of strategic management. However, internal environment of the organization is a quite essential and important from the point of view of the environment analysis. It is the cornerstone of the new and exiting business opportunity analysis too. For instance, the individual life success depends on his innate capabilities like psychological factors, traits and skills. These are to the cope with the environment then will be got success otherwise failure. The survival is the basic elements and success of the business organization, it has depend on its own strengths in terms of resources like money, men, machinery, materials, market and methods as its command. Organization success depends on effective utilization of physical resource, financial resources and human resource skills. These are adaptability to the business environment.

Every business organization principally consists of internal environment factors and set of external environmental factors. In this chapter, we shall discuss only the internal environment of the organization/company. Internal environment factors are generally considered as controllable factors of the organization.

Internal environment factors are important to business like personal (human) resource department marketing department, production department, physical facilities, accounting and finance departments and swot analysis. Therefore, the organization controls over these factors, these factors are modified or alter by the organization that suit for the business environment.

2. **Internal Analysis of the Organization/Company:** Formulation of an effective and efficient strategy has based on a clear definition of organization mission, an accurate assessment of the external environment and through internal analysis of the organization. Organization requires success it needs at least three ingredients. They are as listed:

   ❖ Strategy must be consistent with conditions in the competitive environment.

   ❖ Strategy must place realistic requirements on the organization/company's internal resources and capabilities.

   ❖ Strategy must be carefully formulated, implemented, controllable and executed. Internal analysis of the organization is to difficult and challenging one to strategist.

An internal analysis has leads to design a realistic organization profile. It frequently involves tradeoff, value system judgments, educated and skilled guess as well as objective and standardized analysis. A systematic internal analysis leads to main objective of the organization profile. It is essential to develop strategy and design a realistic mission for achievement of the strategy. Internal analysis of the organization must identify the strategically strengths, opportunities, weakness and threats that are based on organization strategy. Organizational analysis identifies suitable strategy that based on the SWOT analysis. Internal analysis can be achieved by first identifying key internal factors like value system, mission objectives, management structure and nature, integrated power relationship, human resource, company/organization image and brand equity, physical assets, R&D, technological capabilities, marketing resource and financial resource factors and secondly by evaluating these factors.

Steps/Process in the Development of a Organizational/Company Profile

Company/organization profile focus on determination of strengths and weakness of the strategic environment of the business. Identifying and evaluating strategic internal factors are based to accomplish to organization future strategy. The major steps are important to development of an organization/company profile. They are listed below:

Stage one: Identification of Strategic Factors
Stage two: Using Value Chain Analysis
Stage three: Evaluations of strategic internal factors

Levels of Analysis

1. Organizational Analysis: Identification of short- and long-term goals - Identification of human resource needs
    ❖ Evaluation of methods of meeting HR needs (e.g., selection, training)
    ❖ Assessment of resource availability
    ❖ Evaluation of support for transfer of training
2. Task (Job) Analysis
    ❖ Identification of: tasks
    ❖ standards
    ❖ optimal procedures
3. Person Analysis: Evaluation of individual against standards
    ❖ Identification of deficiencies
    ❖ Identification of causes (e.g., motivation vs. ability)
4. Demographic Analysis
    ❖ Assess the specific training needs of various demographic groups (e.g, the disabled)

Ans. 19.

Change management is a set of ideas, strategies, and skills that can be applied to engage change effectively These may be applied in planning for change in implementing change in supporting continuous improvement following change.

Change management methods may be applied to any type of organizational change, including departmental mergers, technology implementation, creating team-based organizations and professional development. It may be helpful to think about change management methods on two levels:

The first level of change management is generic enough to apply to any type of change, whether it's the creation of a new department or the implementation of a new technology. At this generic level, change management methods are mostly targeted at understanding the human response to change and creating effective strategies for engaging people to achieve change.

The second level of change management includes methods that are specific to a particular change. For example, in technology implementations, specific actions include establishing and communicating the business case for change, ongoing relationship building communication and training for affected staff, redesigning business processes, and training for affected staff, redesigning business processes, and creating and sustaining groups to manage the project. While some of these activities apply to other types of change, this collection forms a boilerplate for technology implementation.

Others are

- management development programs
- Organization culture change
- OD interventions
- organization restructuring etc.

Why People Resist Change?

There are many reasons why employees of all sizes/ shapes may react negatively to change.

Personal Loss: People are afraid they will lose something. They might be right or they might be wrong in their fear. Some of the things they might lose are as follows:

Security: They might lose their jobs through a reduction in force or elimination of their jobs.

Automation and a decline in sales often bring about this feeling.

Money: They might lose money through a reduction in salary, pay, benefits, or overtime Or, expenses such as travel may be increased because of a move to another location that is farther from their home.

Pride and satisfaction: They might end up with jobs that no longer require their abilities and skills.

Friends and important contact: They might be moved to another location where they will no longer have contact with friends and important people. This loss of visibility and daily contacts is very serious people who are ambitious as well as those with a strong need for love and acceptance.

Freedom: They might be put on a job under a boss who no longer gives them freedom to do it "their way." Closer supervision that provides less opportunity for decision making is a dramatic loss to some people.

Responsibility: Their jobs might be reduced to menial tasks without responsibility. This may occur when a new boss takes over or through changes in methods or equipment.

Authority: They might lose their position of power and authority over people. This frequently happens when re-organization takes place or when a new boss decides to usurp some of the authority that an individual had.

Good working conditions: They might be moved from a large private office to a small one or to a desk in a work area with only a partition between people.

Status: Their job title, responsibility, or authority might be reduced from an important one to a lesser one with loss of status and recognition from others. This also happens when another layer of management is inserted between a subordinate and manager.

Ans. 20.

1. The company business was run on "Production Oriented" Basis.
   - No market research, [conducted no marketing research continuously-
   - pre-product/during product launch/ during the maturity / consumer research/retail research/test marketing etc.
   - No product planning/development, [they had no plan develop products in a scientific manner, tailoring it to the exact taste of the consumers]
   - No Effective product pricing, [did not conduct price research and position the price point where the consumer can afford/the company makes good profit.]
   - No Effective product marketing [the company conducted no effective product marketing programs]
   - No Effective Sales Programs [the company had no network of sales representatives]
   - No Effective promotion, [the company did not apply varieties of promotions including sales promotion/ trade promotion/consumer promotion/ advertising/ public relations]|
   - No Effective distribution, [when it comes to distribution, they had no an distribution network.
   - No Effective customer care, [the company had no well crafted customer care program for the consumers.]
   - Poor Branding [when it comes to branding, they were no good.
   - POOR merchandising [the company had no program on merchandising like external displays/internal displays]
   - Poor retailing [the company had a poor presence in the retail field]

2. The CEO Suggestions Were Shallow/Ineffective.
   - diluted the marketing effort.
   - was not focused.

The company should tailor its marketing practices

Successful businesses focus on getting the basics of marketing right. Some of the things that the company should do in marketing practices is to:

- Have a marketing team or individuals who have qualifications in marketing
- Review brand, its image and what it stands for
- Consider the consistent use of a strap line in the advertisements

- Launch a website and think about e-marketing and interactive website pages to add value
- Adopt the correct pricing strategy for the market sector, competitors, customers & profit
- Create a database of all the retailers so that you can market to them again
- Know your consumers find out where they are spending time and money
- Employ specialists for website creation or use external experts in the field
- Use external professionals for press releases
- Support anyone wanting to train in marketing
- Have a consistent brand message on all literature, websites, business cards & letter heads
- Create a mission statement
- Always plan properly, there are packages such as Micros oft Project which can help
- Use market research to understand competitors, spot opportunities and lessen risks
- Use the database to market either by postal campaigns, e-mail or even mobile marketing
- Advertise in the correct places, and analyse and learn from each campaign
- Enlist professional designers for literature, business cards and logos
- Stick to what you do best and let the experts help with their specialist knowledge.

"MBA BASICS IN 24 HOURS!"

Both kindle version & Paperback.

10 Books! Available in Amazon now!

Principles & Practices of Management,
Human Resource Management, Financial Management,
Marketing Management, Organizational Behaviour,
Managerial Economics, Strategic Management & MIS.
+PMP/Proj Management & International Business/Foreign Trade

Search the above title in Amazon

Ans. 21

Career planning system for employees is an outcome of career management process. Which is an outcome of
- corporate strategic planning
- corporate objectives
- corporate strategy

Succession planning, is an element of career management process. Career Planning is a critical element/outcome of
1. Succession planning,
2. Performance appraisal and
3. "Potential" assessment systems.

Career planning- the competency band approach

It is possible to define career progression in terms of the competencies required by individuals to carry out work at progressive levels of responsibility or contribution. These levels can be described as competency bands. Competencies would be defined as the attributes and behavioral characteristics needed to perform effectively at each discrete level in a job or career family. The number of levels would vary according to the range of competencies required in a particular job family. For each band, the experience and training needed to achieve the competency level would be defined. These definitions would provide a career map incorporating aiming points for individuals, who would be made aware of the competency levels they must reach in order to achieve progress in their careers This would help them to plan their own development, although support and guidance should be provided by their managers, and HR specialists. The provision of additional experience and training could be arranged as appropriate, but it would be important to clarify what individual employees need to do for themselves if they want to progress within the organization. The advantage of this approach is that people are provided with aiming points and an understanding of what they need to do to reach them. One of the major causes of frustration and job dissatisfaction is the absence of this information.

A competency band career development approach can be linked to Aiming points

1. Career counseling Performance management processes, should provide for counseling sessions between individuals and their managers. These sessions should give the former the opportunity to discuss their aspirations and the latter the chance to comment on them

- ❖ helpfully
- ❖ and, at a later stage, to put forward specific career development proposals to be fed into the overall career management programs.

2. Personal development planning Personal development planning is carried out by individuals with guidance, encouragement and help from their managers/HRM as required. A personal development plan sets out the actions people propose to take to learn and to develop themselves. They take responsibility for formulating and implementing the plan, but they receive support from the organization and their managers in doing so. The purpose is to provide a 'self-organized learning framework'

3. Management development: Formal approaches to management development The formal approaches to management development include: *development on the job through coaching, counseling, monitoring and feedback by managers on a continuous basis associated with the use of performance management processes to identify and satisfy development needs, and with mentoring; *development through work experience, which includes job rotation, job enlargement, taking part in project teams or task groups, 'action learning', and secondment outside the organization; *formal training by means of internal or external courses; *structured self-development by following self-managed learning contract with the manager or a management development adviser - these may include guidance reading or the deliberate extension of knowledge or acquisition of new skills on the job.

Mentoring:

Mentoring is the process of using specially selected and trained individuals to provide guidance and advice which will help to develop the careers of the 'proteges' Allocated to them. Mentoring is aimed at complementing learning on the job, which must always be the best way of acquiring the particular skills and knowledge the job holder needs. Mentoring also complements formal training by providing those who benefit from it with individual guidance from experienced managers who are 'wise in the ways of the organization'. Mentors provide for the person or persons allocated to them : advice in drawing up self-development programs or learning contracts: general help with learning programs; guidance on how to acquire the necessary knowledge and skills to do a new job; advice on dealing with any administrative, technical or people problems individuals meet.

Ans. 22.

Different work practices which promote learning:

<u>First Set of Work Practices.</u>

At least four key steps are involved in creating a strong learning" climate. They involve understanding and respecting the adult learner and creating a positive consultant/client relationship:

1. Recognise that participants in your programme should ultimately take their learning to their "real world", and that most of the responsibility for making it work in the application environment must be theirs.

2. Acknowledge specifically and at the beginning of your programme, that the responsibility for programme success must be shared - that you have organised the information (experiences) to respond as closely as possible to the needs of the group but that each individual must modify as necessary to make the information relevant and to apply it in the "real world". Design, in other words, is a shared process, requiring that the educator:

Analyse group needs. Find information. Organise information. Present information. Facilitate learning. But that the learner: Analyse their own needs. Customise objectives to those needs. Adjust the application environment to make it congenial to the new behaviours. Apply the learning.

3. Design activities that encourage learners to clarify their own objectives and that help them plan application.

4. Create an adult problem-solving climate in the "classroom" by planning a design that allows you to interact with learners as a counsellor/consultant would. Your design should allow you to: Create a physical environment that encourages sharing and reduces barriers between the educator and the learners. Be empathic- showing you understand their situation, needs, feelings. Respect the learners and their attempts to contribute. Be yourself - without defensiveness, hidden agenda, or pseudo professionalism - sharing yourself and your experiences when they can illustrate ideas or help establish empathy. Focus on the learner's needs and problems not on retro fitting solutions. Confront and challenge - but only after empathy and respect have been established (this makes it less likely that learners will be defensive). Such a climate encourages learners to feel cared for, safe, understood, real, responsible and strong. It helps open dialogue and analysis channels. In short, along with the other steps it facilitates the motivation to learn.

Second Set of Work Practices.

Knowledge Acquisition

Learning occurs when an organization acquires knowledge. Acquisition of declarative knowledge or facts and information is achieved by monitoring the environment, using information systems to store, manage, and retrieve information, carrying out research and development, carrying out education and training, patent watching, and bibliometrics. Learning occurs not only due to knowledge acquisition from outside the organization but also due to the rearrangement of existing knowledge, the revision of previous knowledge structures, and the building and revision of theories. Information Distribution: Information distribution refers to the process by which an organization shares information among its units and members, thereby promoting learning and producing new knowledge or understanding. Knowledge in the form of tacit know-how, letters, memos, informal conversations, and reports are captured and distributed. A lot of learning and innovation takes place in informal "communities of practice". Very often, learning in an organization takes place by members sharing stories or anecdotes of actual work practice as opposed to what is mentioned in formal job descriptions or procedure manuals. Greater sharing or distribution of information leads to greater organizational learning. Information Interpretation: In order for information to be shared, such information must be interpreted.

Third Set of Work Practices

1. Performance appraisal and individual development plan helps the learning/development of the individuals.
2. Effective talent management programs too help to learn/ develop individuals with potential.

Fourth Set of Work Practices

An effective job design includes

Job Enlargement: Job enlargement changes the jobs to include more and/or different tasks. Job enlargement should add interest to the work but may or may not give employees more
responsibility.

Job Rotation: Job rotation moves employees from one task to another. It distributes the group tasks among a number of employees.

Job Enrichment: Job enrichment allows employees to assume more responsibility, accountability, and independence when learning new tasks or to allow for greater participation and new opportunities.

Job Engineering Work design allows employees to see how the work methods, layout and handling procedures link together as well as the interaction between people and machines.

Induction: a good/effective induction helps to learn better/faster and make the entry to the company more easy/warm.

Orientation: a good/effective orientation helps to learn better/orientate faster and make the entry to the job position more easier.

Fifth Set of Work Practices.

Practice Inclusivity-Individual differences with particular needs are acknowledged, respected and valued.

Personal perceptions and attitudes about difference are examined and revised to improve communication and professionalism

Principles underpinning inclusivity are integrated into all work practices

The training and/or assessment organisation's access and equity policy is used to guide work practices Individuals' rights and confidentiality are respected.

Sixth Set of Work Practices

Promote and Respond to Diversity

The ground rules for participation and behaviour with colleagues and clients are established through a cooperative, agreed process. Individuals are encouraged to express themselves and to contribute to the work and learning environment, Individuals are provided with opportunities to indicate specific needs to support their participation in learning and work.

Seventh Set of Work Practices

It Develop and Implement Work Strategies to Support Inclusively.

Documented resources to support and guide inclusive practices are identified and used to inform work strategies. Support persons are identified and included in the work and learning process where appropriate and agreed to.

Relevant professional support services are identified and accessed, as appropriate. Any physical environment support needs are acknowledged and incorporated into work practices, where practicable and approved by appropriate personnel.

Eighth Set of Work Practices

It Promote a Culture of Learning. Support and advice is provided to colleagues and clients to encourage new and ongoing participation in learning opportunities. It is through learning, individuals improve - develop their career and the outcomes of the organization.

Ans. 23.

The phenomenal growth of private sector of India can be attributed to
- political will,
- financial reforms,
- usage of more advanced technology,
- young and large English speaking working class.

The 7-8 % of annual GDP growth rate India is the one of the highest growth rate in the world. The last 15 years witnessed a phenomenal rise of the growth of private sector in India. The opening up of Indian economy has led to free inflow of foreign direct investment (FDI) along with modern cutting edge technology, which propelled India's economic growth.

Previously, the Indian market were ruled by the government enterprises but the scene in Indian market changed as soon as the markets were opened for investments. This saw the rise of the Indian private companies which prioritized customer's need and speedy service. This further fueled competition amongst same industry players and even in government organizations. Further, the government of India also divested some of its enterprises to ensure smooth operation of these companies which was otherwise were loss making. It also went further and forged joint venture private Indian companies, especially in sectors like, telecommunication, petroleum, housing and infrastructure. This inculcated healthy competition and benefited the end consumers, since the cost of service or products come down substantially.

Medium grade private Indian companies are also offering lucrative and competitively priced products or service, whose quality is at par with A grade companies. Big players of Indian markets have been forced to lower their price bands to remain

alive in the competition. Further, these big private Indian companies are offering mouth watering benefits in the form of gifts, rebates and even holding lucky draws to stay ahead in the race of 'market supremacy'. Gone are the days when 'brand loyalty, accounted for big customer base. Today, general Indian customers are trendy, flexible and are extremely flexible with their choice. Steady growth of private sector has sent a sense of urgency and insecurity amongst main market players. Defensive methods of protection of Brands against competitors are becoming popular.

Legal instruments like patents, trademarks, industrial designs and copyrights filing has increased many
fold and so is counter claim and litigation. Further, Mergers and Acquisitions, collaborations and licensing has become a popular amongst private Indian companies.

The best thing that has happened to the overall Indian market with the growth of private sector is that it has helped to shed bureaucracy and lengthy official process and supplemented it by customer eccentric service, good work ethics, professionalism and transparency of accounts.

Some positive effect of the growth of private sector in India are as follows - Manufacturing registered 11.9 % growth The passenger vehicles sector grew by 11.61% during April-May 2007 Electricity, gas & water supply performed well and recorded an impressive growth rate of 8.3% Construction growth rate rose to 10.7 % Trade, hotels, transport and communication registered a growth rate of 12% Financing, insurance, real estate and business services recorded an impressive growth rate of at 11% during the 1st quarter of this fiscal Exports grew by 18.11% during the 1st quarter of 2007-2008 and the imports shoot up by 34.30 % during the same period The food sector is estimated to be of US$ 200 billion and it is expected to grow to $310 billion by 2015 Merchandise Exports recorded strong growth.

Ans. 24.

A network is a collection of computers and devices connected to each other. The network allows computers to communicate with each other and share resources and information. The Advance Research Projects Agency (ARPA) designed "Advanced Research Projects Agency Network" (ARPANET) for the United States Department of Defense. It was the first computer network in the world in late 1960's and early 1970's.

Basic Hardware Components

All networks are made up of basic hardware building blocks to interconnect network nodes, such as Network Interface Cards (NICS), Bridges, Hubs, Switches, and Routers. In addition, some method of connecting these building blocks is required, usually in the form of galvanic cable (most commonly Category 5 cable). Less common are microwave links (as in IEEE 802.12) or optical cable ('optical fiber). An ethernet card may also be required.

Network interface cards (Network Card)

A network card, network adapter or NIC (network interface card) is a piece of computer hardware designed to allow computers to communicate over a computer network. It provides physical access to a networking medium and often provides a low level addressing system through the use of MAC addresses.

Repeaters

A repeater is an electronic device that receives a signal and retransmits it at a higher power level, or to the other side of an obstruction, so that the signal can cover longer distances without degradation. In most twisted pair Ethernet configurations, repeaters are required for cable which runs longer than 100 meters.

Hubs

A hub contains multiple ports. When a packet arrives at one port, it is copied unmodified to all ports of the hub for transmission. The destination address in the frame is not changed to a broadcast address.

Bridges (Network bridge)

A network bridge connects multiple network segments at the data link layer (layer 2) of the OSI model. Bridges do not promiscuously copy traffic to all ports, as hubs do, but learn which MAC addresses are reachable through specific ports. Once the bridge associates a port and an address, it will send traffic for that address only to that port. Bridges do send broadcasts to all ports except the one on which the broadcast was received.

Bridges learn the association of ports and addresses by examining the source address of frames that it sees on various ports. Once a frame arrives through a port, its source address is stored and the bridge assumes that MAC address is associated with that port. The first time that a previously unknown destination address is seen, the bridge will
forward the frame to all ports other than the one on which the frame arrived.

Bridges come in three basic types:
1. Local bridges: Directly connect local area networks (LANS)
2. Remote bridges: Can be used to create a wide area network (WAN) link between LANS. Remote bridges, where the connecting link is slower than the end networks, largely have been replaced by routers.

3. Wireless bridges: Can be used to join LANS or connect remote stations to LANS.

Switches (Network switch)

A switch is a device that forwards and filters OSI layer 2 datagrams (chunk of data communication) between ports(connected cables) based on the MAC addresses in the packets. This is distinct from a hub in that it only forwards the packets to the ports involved in the communications rather than all ports corunected. Strictly speaking, a switch is not capable of routing traffic based on IP address (OSI Layer 3) which is necessary for communicating between network segments or within a large or complex LAN. Some switches are capable of routing based on IP addresses but are still called switches as a marketing term. A switch normally has numerous ports, with the intention being that most or all of the network is connected directly to the switch, or another switch that is in turn connected to a switch.

Switch is a marketing term that encompasses routers and bridges, as well as devices that may distribute traffic on load or by application content (e.g., a Web URL identifier). Switches may operate at one or more OSI model layers, including physical,

data link, network, or transport(i.e., end-to-ernd). A device that operates simultaneously at more than one of these layers is called a multilayer switch.

Overemphasizing the ill-defined term "switch" often leads to confusion when first trying to understand networking. Many experienced network designers and operators recommend starting with the logic of devices dealing with only one protocol level, not all of which are covered by OSI. Multilayer device selection is an advanced topic that may lead to selecting particular implementations, but multilayer switching is simply not a real world design concept.

Routers

Routers are networking devices that forward data packets between networks using headers and forwarding tables to determine the best path to forward the packets.

Routers work at the network layer.

Ans. 25.

Portfolio analysis is necessary of the elements of a firm's product mix to determine the optimum allocation of its resources. Two most common measures used in a portfolio analysis are
- market growth rate and
- relative market share.

Product portfolio strategy

The business portfolio is the collection of businesses and products that make up the company. The best business portfolio is one that fits the company's strengths and helps exploit the most attractive opportunities.

The company must:

1. Analyse its current business portfolio and decide which businesses should receive more or less investment, and

2. Develop growth strategies for adding new products and businesses to the portfolio, whilst at the same time deciding when products and businesses should no longer be retained.

The Boston Consulting Group Box ("BCG Box")

Using the BCG Box, a company classifies all its business units according to two dimensions: On the horizontal axis: relative market share-this serves as a measure of SBU strength in the market On the vertical axis: market growth rate - this provides a measure of market attractiveness By dividing the matrix into four areas, four types of SBU can be distinguished:

Stars: Stars are high growth businesses or products competing in markets where they are relatively strong compared with the competition. Often they need heavy investment to sustain their growth. Eventually their growth will slow and, assuming they maintain their relative market share, will become cash cows.

Cash Cows: Cash cows are low-growth businesses or products with a relatively high market share. These are mature, successful businesses with relatively little need for investment. They need to be managed for continued profit – so that they continue to generate the strong cash flows that the company needs for its Stars.

Question marks: Question marks are businesses or products with low market share but which operate in higher growth markets. This suggests that they have potential, but may require substantial investment in order to grow market share at the expense of more powerful competitors. Management have to think hard about question marks" - Which ones should they invest in? which ones they allow to fail or shrink?

Dogs: Unsurprisingly, the term "dogs" refers to businesses or products that have low relative share in unattractive, low-growth markets. Dogs may generate enough cash to break-even, but they are rarely, if ever, worth investing in

Using the BCG Box to determine strategy

Once a company has classified its SBU's, it must decide what to do with them. In the diagram above, the company has one large cash cow (the size of the circle is proportional to the SBU's sales), a large dog and two, smaller stars and question marks.

Conventional strategic thinking suggests there are four possiblee strategies for each SBU:

1. Build Share: here the company can invest to increase market share (for example turning a "question mark" into a star)

2. Hold: here the company invests just enough to keep the SBU in its present position

3. Harvest: here the company reduces the amount of investment in order to maximise the short-term cash flows and profits from the SBU. This may have the effect of turning Stars into Cash Cows.

4. Divest: the company can divest the SBU by phasing it out or selling it- in order to use the resources elsewhere (e-g. investing in the more promising 'question marks").

Ans. 26.

One of the main challenges that small and mid-sized businesses face is managing and caring for their employees. Factoring in payroll, taxes, and insurance costs, employee-related costs can be one of a company's largest expenses.

During recent years, Professional Employer Organizations (PEOS) have become a viable new way for smaller companies to save money on their human resources costs. A PEO manages all your employee-related functions payroll, taxes, insurance very cost effectively, freeing you to focus on your business.

Once you hire employees, you are required to pay them a salary, pay unemployment fees, and take out workers' compensation insurance. Depending on the number of employees, larger companies normally delegate employee-related functions to a dedicated human resources department. But what should a company do when it has too few employees to justify creating a formal HR department?

This problem has given rise to HR outsourcing firms that companies contract with to take over certain employee-related tasks. Outsourcing takes the HR burden off smaller businesses and transfers them to an outside firm that specializes in the various areas of human resources: payroll administration, benefits, and employee orientation and training. The benefits HR outsourcing can offer include:

- Skilled professionals to do the job
- Improved employee relations

Money saved by cutting overall expenses A PEO takes the concept of HR outsourcing one step further. Rather than specializing in certain areas, a PEO becomes the employer of record, and as such takes on all legal responsibilities for your employees. In practice, the PEO will legally hire all of your current employees, making it responsible for taxes and insurance. When you hire a PEO, you enter into a contract that defines

1. Powers,
2. responsibilities, and
3. liabilities: The services of a PEO come under four basic headings.

These are: o Payroll. Mainly this involves keeping track of employee work time, deducting federal and state taxes, and issuing checks.

Human Resources Compliance: Ensuring that all of your employee procedures comply with federal and state laws, including race or gender discrimination laws.

Benefits Administration: This can include things such as health benefits, vacation, sick leave, and retirement.

Risk Management: A vital area that has to do with insurance, primarily workers' compensation insurance. Although sometimes aligned with temporary employment agencies and staff leasing firms, a PEO provides a much different type of service. Unlike a temp agency, your employees are intended to be permanent and not moved around to a variety of different jobs. In terms of staff leasing, you are not just leasing any employee, you're leasing your own employee. Everything is the same, except that your employee receives his or her checks and benefits from an outside firm. The employees still work for you, but all their taxes, benefits, and insurance are handled by an outside source. A PEO can save your company money. For example, a PEO can offer you the advantages of group insurance. They can do this because they handle a variety of small businesses that they pool together, getting better rates for all businesses involved. When looking for a PEO, do some comparison shopping as to their differing fees and responsibilities.

Ans. 27.

Performance appraisal, also known as employee appraisal, is a method by which the job performance of an employee is evaluated (generally in terms of quality, quantity, cost and time). Performance appraisal is a part of career development. Perfermance appraisals are regular reviews of employee performance within organizations Generally, the aims of a performance appraisal are to:

1. Give feedback on performance to employees.
2. Identify employee training needs.
3. Document criteria used to allocate organizational rewards
4. Form a basis for personnel decisions: salary increases, promotions, disciplinary actions, etc.
5. Provide the opportunity for organizational diagnosis and development.
6. Facilitate communication between employee and administrator.
7. Validate selection techniques and human resource policies to meet federal.

Equal Employment Opportunity requirements: A common approach to assessing performance is to use a numerical or scalar rating system whereby managers are asked to score an individual against a number of objectives/attributes. In some companies, employees receive assessments from their manager, peers, subordinates and customers while also performing a self assessment. This is known as 360° appraisal. The most popular methods that are being used as performance appraisal process are:

1. Management by objectives
2. 360 degree appraisal
3. Behavioral Observation Scale
4. Behaviorally Anchored Rating Scale Trait based systems, which rely on factors such as integrity and conscientiousness, are also commonly used by businesses. The scientific literature on the subject provides evidence that assessing employees on factors such as these should be avoided. The reasons for this are two-fold:

(i) Trait based systems are by definition based on personality traits, they make it difficult for a manager to provide feedback that can cause positive change in employee performance.

This is caused by the fact that personality dimensions are for the most part static, and while an employee can change a specific behavior they cannot change their personality. For example, a person who lacks integrity may stop lying to a manager because they have been caught, but they still have low integrity and are likely to lie again when the threat of being caught is gone .

(ii) Trait based systems are vague, are more easily influenced by office politics, causing, them to be less reliable as a source of information on an employee's true performance. The vagueness of these instruments allows managers to fill them out based on who they want to/feel should get a raise, rather than basing scores on specific behaviors employees should/should not be engaging, in. These systems are also more likely to leave a company open to discrimination claims because a manager can make biased decisions without having to back them up with specific behavioral information.

Ans. 28.

The following are the areas in an organization where knowledge management (KM) can be used to make it more competitive.

1. KM can help to manage the critical issues/hence the competitiveness [the issues that needs constant attention to grow the business] how can we manage the critical issues affecting the organization
2. KM can help strengthen the drivers of company performance/hence the competitiveness [critical elements that help to grow the company business like R & D]
how can we manage the drivers for excellent performance
3. KM can help to develop the keys of success/hence the competitiveness [keys which helps the success of the company like training/development] how can we increase the profit level/profitability, using the drivers.
4. KM can help the HR department functions to be more competitive
5. KM can help the marketing department functions to be more competitive
   ❖ Market Geographics using KM.
6. KM can help the Pricing Functions to be more competitive [by helping to devise price/ trade terms in the market KM can increase the effectiveness of the Pricing Function and make significant contribution to the competitiveness.
7. KM can help the Distribution Function to be more competitive. [by helping to devise strategies/plans to improve channel penetration] KM can increase the effectiveness of the Distribution Function and Increase the Market Coverage/make significant contribution to the competitiveness.
8. KM can help the Sales Function to be more competitive.
   ❖ sales objectives [by helping to direct the sales team and get the sales volume]
   ❖ sales target [by helping to set sales team target and improve performance]
   ❖ sales forecast [by helping sales planning and development] KM can increase the effectiveness of the Sales Function and Increase the Customer Coverage/make significant contribution to the competitiveness.
9. KM can help the Promotion Mix to be more competitive.
   ❖ Marketing Communicaton Objectives (by helping to maximise the awareness of products]

- ❖ Sales Promotion Objectives [by helping to create better impact at the point of sale/customers]
- ❖ Advertising Objectives [by helping to maximise the media coverage]
- ❖ Public Relations Objectives [by helping to improve the company image in the community/market] KM can increase the Marketing Mix Effectiveness and make significant contribution to the competitiveness

10. KM can help the Manufacturing function to be more competitive
    - ❖ production objectives [by helping to improve the production effectiveness/efficiency]
    - ❖ raw material inventory levels [by helping to control the holding cost]
    - ❖ finished goods inventory levels [by helping to meet the sales requirements and control holding cost]
    - ❖ warehousing objectives [by helping to improve the warehousing operation effectiveness/efficiency]
    - ❖ customer service objectives [by helping to improve the customer satisfaction level] KM can improve the manufacturing process/and the productivity and hence make significant contribution to the competitiveness.

11. KM can help the purchase function to be more competitive.
    - ❖ purchase dept objectives [by helping to keep the production level/remove material shortages]
    - ❖ purchases cost [by helping to economise the purchases] KM can improve the procurement effectiveness and reduce costs and hence make significant contribution to the competitiveness

All the above steps help to make the organization competitive and help to make healthy.

Ans. 29.

The Advantages (Benefits) of Networking

You have undoubtedly heard the "the whole is greater than the sum of its parts". This phrase describes networking very well, and explain why it has become so popular. A network isn't a bunch of computers with wires running between them. Properly implemented, a network is a system that provides its users with unique capabilities, above and beyond what the individual machines and their software applications can provide.

Most of the benefits of networking can be divided into two generic categories: connectivity and sharing. Networks allow computers, and hence their users, to be connected together. They also allow for the easy sharing of information and resources, and cooperation between the devices in other ways. Since modern business depends so much on the intelligent flow and management of information, this tells you a lot about why networking is so valuable.

Here, in no particular order, are some of the specific advantages generally associated with networking:

- Connectivity annd Comunmication: Networks connect computers and the users of those computers. Individuals within a building or work group can be connected into local area networks (LANS); LANS in distant locations can be interconnected into larger wide area networks (WANS). Once connected, it is possible for network users to communicate with each other using technologies such as electronic mail. This makes the transmission of business(or non-business) information easier, more efficient and less expensive than it would be without the network.

- Data Sharing: One of the most important uses of networking is to allow the sharing of data. Before networking was common, an accounting employee who wanted to prepare a report for her manager would have to produce it on his PC, put it on a floppy disk, and then walk it over to the manager who would transfer the data, such PC's hard disk. (This sort of shoe-based network" was sometimes sarcastically called a "sneakernet".)

- True networking allows thousands of employees to share data much more easily and quickly than this. More so, it makes possible applications that rely on the ability of many people to access and share the same data, such as databases, group software development, and much more. Intranets and extranets can be used

to distribute corporate information between sites and to business partners.
- Hardware Sharing Networks facilitate the sharing of hardware devices. For example, instead of giving each of 10 employees in a department an expensive color printer (or resorting to the "sneakernet again), one printer can be placed on the network for everyone to share.
- Internet Access: The Internet is itself an enormous network, so whenever you access the Internet, you are using a network. The significance of the Internet on modern society is hard to exaggerate, especially for those of us in technical fields.
- Internet Access Sharing Small computer networks allow multiple users to share a single Internet connection. Special hardware devices allow the bandwidth of the connection to be easily allocated to various individuals as they need it, and permit an organization to purchase one high-speed connection instead of many slower ones.
- Data Security and Management: In a business environment, a network allows the administrators to much better manage the company's critical data. Instead of having this data spread over dozens or even hundreds of small computers in a haphazard fashion as their users create it, data can be centraliged on shared servers. This makes it easy for everyone to find the data, makes it possible for the administrators to ensure that the data is regularly backed up, and also allows for the implementation of security measures to control who can read or change various pieces of critical information.
- Performance Enhancement and Balancing: Under some circumstances, a network can be used to enhance overall performance of some applications by distributing the computation tasks to various computers on the network.

Entertainment :Networks facilitate many types of games and entertainment. The Intermet itself offers many sources of entertainment, of course. In addition, many multi-player games exist that operate over a local area network. Many home networks are set up for this reason, and gaming across wide area networks (including the Internet) has also become quite popular. Of course, if you are running a business and have easily-amused employees, you might insist that this is really a disadvantage of networking and not an advantage.

Ans.30.

Classical approach to management

Classical looks at organizations in terms of purpose & formal structure Emphasis was placed on the planning of work, technical requirements of the organization, principles of management, and the assumption of rational and logical behavior A clear understanding of the purpose of the organization was essential to understand how the

organization works and how its working methods can be improved.

Common principles to the classical approach to management

Principle of coordination: the need for people to act together with unity of action, and need for discipline

The scalar principle: the hierarchy of organizaton, the grading of duties and process of delegation

Functional principle: specialization & distinction between different kinds of duties

Criticisms of the classical approach

Insufficient account taken of personality factors Creates organizational structures where people can exercise only limited control over their work environment Out-of-date approach

(a) Scientific Management

There is a best machine for each job, so there is a best working method by which people should undertake their jobs All job processes should be analysed into discrete tasks & via this management find the 'one best way to perform each task.

Principles of scientific management

The development of a true science for each person's work The scientific selection, training and development of workers Co-operation with workers to ensure work is carried out in prescribed way The division of work and responsibility between management and workers

Bureaucracy- the main characteristics

Tasks are allocated as official duties among the various positions An implied clear-cut division of labour and a high level of specialisation Uniformity of decisions and actions achieved through formally established systems of rules & regulations An impersonal orientation expected from officials in their dealing with clients Employment is based on technical qualifications.

Bureaucracy - the main features
- Specialisation
- Hierarchy of authority
- System of rules
- Impersonality

Criticism of bureaucracy

Over-emphasis on rules and procedures, record keeping and paperwork Lack of flexibility and stifling of initiative Position and responsibilities can lead to officious bureaucratic behaviour Impersonal relations can lead to stereotyped behaviour
and lack of responsiveness to individual incidents or problems

(b) Human Relations Approach

Is based on the consideration of the social factors at work and the behaviour of employees within an organization Particular importance is paid to the informal organization and the satisfaction of individuals' needs through groups at work Hawthorne experiments acted as a turning point in the development of the Human Relations movement.

Human relations approach-the criticisms

Weak methodology of Hawthorne experiments, including failure to take sufficient account of environmental factors Adoption of a management approach, a 'unitary frame of reference' and over simplification of theories Insufficiently scientific and takes too narrow a view, ignoring the role of the organization within society.

(c) The Systems Approach

Attempts to reconcile the classical and human relations approaches Attention is focused on: the total work of the organization the inter-relationships of structures & behavior the range of variables within the organization The organization is viewed within its total environment and the importance of multiple channels in interaction is
emphasized.

(d) The contingency approach

Views the structure of an orgganization and its success as dependent on: the nature of tasks that are undertaken the nature of environmental influences There is no one best way to structure or manage organizations it is dependent on the contingencies of the situation.

(e) Post modernism
A more recent view of organizations and management Rejects a rational, systems approach and accepted explanations of society and behavior Places greater emphasis on the use of language and attempts to portray a particular set of assumptions or versions of the truth Advantages of different approaches/categorizations Provides a setting, in which to view the field of management.

Traces the major lines of argument developed by different writers Provides a framework in which principles can be set and comparisons of management practice made Helps in organizational analysis and identification of problem areas Enables managers to select those ideas which best suit the requirements of their job.

Author : G R Narasimhan

CONCLUSION

- This additional book under <u>MBA Basics in 24 Hours Q & A</u> helps you to get quick knowledge of complete set of masters in business administration questions and related or suggested answers.
- Short, simple summary & keywords answers can be used to present the whole topic in just less than three hours.
- The ideas/ questions and definitions/answers can be used for examinations, viva, interviews, knowledge sharing/transfer & also certification too!
- Group discussions can be arranged and the above Q&As are really helpful to bring out the best members in management.
- Examination papers can be set at the required levels in simple terms.
- The given information in all the chapters can also be used in schools, colleges/ universities, industries or corporate sectors and any other levels.
- Other books under "MBA Basics in 24 hours" are also given in the same way to help out best for students and tutors (published in Amazon).
  - Principles & Practices of Management
  - Human Resource Management
  - Financial Management
  - Marketing Management
  - Organizational Behavior
  - Managerial Economics
  - Strategic Management
  - Management Information Systems

- Additionally "Global Marketing and Foreign Trade" & "Project Management PMP/CAPM" books were published. You can get all these books in Amazon. Book names with author name "G R Narasimhan"!

For any feedback, query or suggestions please mail to astronara@gmail.com or info@zodiacservices.net

You can also contact via www.zodiacservices.net/contact

THANK YOU!

www.ingramcontent.com/pod-product-compliance
Lightning Source LLC
Chambersburg PA
CBHW030652220526
45463CB00005B/1744